Capturing Globalization

D1824910

Edited by James H. Mittelman and Norani Othman

London and New York

First published 2001
by Routledge
11 New Fetter Lane, London EC4P 4EE

Simultaneously published in the USA and Canada
by Routledge
29 West 35th Street, New York, NY 10001

Routledge is an imprint of the Taylor & Francis Group

Typeset in Sabon by Taylor & Francis Books Ltd
Printed and bound in Great Britain by TJ International Ltd, Padstow,
Cornwall

British Library Cataloguing in Publication Data
A catalogue record for this book is available from the British Library

Library of Congress Cataloging-in-Publication Data
Capturing globalization / edited by James H. Mittelman and Norani
Othman.
  p. cm.
Includes bibliographical references and index.
1. International economic relations. 2. Malaysia–Economic
conditions. 3. Globalization. I. Mittelman, James H. II. Norani
Othman.
HF1359 .C3689 2001
337–dc21   2001019133

ISBN 0–415–25732–8 (hbk)
ISBN 0–415–25831–6 (pbk)

Contents

Tables

Contributors

Abdul Rahman Embong, Associate Professor in the Department of Anthropology and Sociology, National University of Malaysia (Universiti Kebangsaan Malaysia), is an Associate Fellow of the Institute of Malaysian and International Studies (IKMAS) and Chief Editor of *Akademika*, the social science journal of Universiti Kebangsaan Malaysia. He has edited four books and his book manuscript on the middle class in Malaysia will be published by Macmillan (forthcoming).

Ishak Shari, Professor of Development Studies, is the Director of the Institute of Malaysian and International Studies (IKMAS), Universiti Kebangsaan Malaysia. He continues to do research on poverty and income distribution, particularly on the implications of globalization for these problems. He is the author or co-author of four books, including *The Fishing Economy: Capital Accumulation, Technological Change and Economic Differentiation* (in Bahasa Malaysia, 1990) and *Development Policies and Income Inequality in Peninsular Malaysia* (with Jomo K.S., 1986).

Clive S. Kessler, Professor of Sociology in the School of Sociology, University of New South Wales, Sydney, Australia, previously taught at the London School of Economics and Political Science (University of London) and Barnard College, Columbia University. Since the mid-1960s he has researched and written extensively about patterns of change in Malay society, culture and politics as well as on social theory generally. He is the author of *Islam and Politics in a Malay State: Kelantan 1838–1969* (Cornell University Press, 1978) and of *Hannah Arendt: Thinking, Judging, Freedom* (Allen and Unwin 1989, co-edited with Gisela Kaplan). He is an international Associate Fellow of the Institute of Malaysian and International Studies (IKMAS).

James H. Mittelman, Professor in the School of International Service, American University, held the Pok Rafeah Chair in International Studies and served as Distinguished Visiting Professor at the Institute of Malaysian and International Studies (IKMAS), Universiti Kebangsaan Malaysia, from 1997 to 1999. His most recent books are, as editor and contributor, *Globalization: Critical Reflections* (Lynne Rienner Publishers, 1996); as co-author, *Out from Underdevelopment Revisited: Changing Global Structures and the Remaking of the Third World* (Macmillan, London and St. Martin's Press, New York, 1997); as co-editor and contributor, *Innovation and Transformation in International Studies* (Cambridge University Press, 1997); and as author, *The Globalization Syndrome: Transformation and Resistance* (Princeton University Press, 2000), which is being translated into Chinese and Japanese.

Norani Othman, Associate Professor and Fellow at the Institute of Malaysian and International Studies (IKMAS) since 1995, was a lecturer at the Department of Anthropology and Sociology, Universiti Kebangsaan Malaysia, from 1976 to 1997. She is the editor of and contributor to two books: *Shari'a Law and the Modern Nation-State: A Malaysian Symposium* (1994) and *Gender, Culture and Religion: Equal before God, Unequal before Man* (co-edited with Cecilia Ng) in 1995. Her most recent publication is 'Grounding Human Rights Arguments in Non-Western Culture: Shari'a and the Citizenship Rights of Women in a Modern Islamic Nation-State', in *The East Asian Challenge for Human Rights*, ed. Joanne R. Bauer and Daniel A. Bell (Cambridge University Press, 1999).

Rajah Rasiah, currently on secondment as Dean of the Faculty of Economics, Universiti Malaysia Sarawak, is Professor of Economics and Fellow at the Institute of Malaysian and International Studies (IKMAS). He was a lecturer at the Department of Economic Analysis, Universiti Kebangsaan Malaysia, since 1991. He pursues research on industrial organizations and trade, foreign investment and industrial transformation, and on globalization and technological development. His publications include two books: *Social and Environmental Clauses and Free Trade: Europe and Southeast Asia* (co-edited with Norbert von Hofmann, published by Friedrich Ebert Stiftung and in Malaysia by Vinlin Press, Petaling

Jaya, 1996) and *Foreign Capital and Industrialization in Malaysia* (Macmillan, London and St Martin's Press, New York, 1996).

Sabihah Osman, Professor and Fellow at the Institute of Malaysian and International Studies (IKMAS), was also Professor of History in the Department of History, Universiti Kebangsaan Malaysia, from 1994 to 1997. She was a lecturer at the department from 1974 to 1994. Her research includes a study of international borders in Southeast Asia, and studies of politics and public administration in Sabah, Sarawak and Brunei. Among her publications are 'Sabah State Elections: Implications for Malaysian Unity', *Asian Survey* XXXII(4), April, 1992; *Sejarah Brunei Menjelang Kemerdekaan* (co-authored with Mohd Hadi Abdullah and Sabullah Haji Hakip, DBP: Kuala Lumpur, 1995), and 'Japanese Economics Activities in Sabah 1890s until 1941', *Journal of Southeast Asian Studies* (National University of Singapore, 1998). She has also completed various consultancy research projects for Malaysian government departments.

Sumit K. Mandal is Research Fellow at the Institute of Malaysian and International Studies (IKMAS), Universiti Kebangsaan Malaysia. He completed his doctoral dissertation 'Finding Their Place: A History of Arabs in Java under Dutch Rule, 1800–1924' at Columbia University, New York in 1994. He wrote the foreword to *Hoakiau di Indonesia* (Chinese in Indonesia [1998]) by the Indonesian author Pramoedya Ananta Toer. His primary areas of research are ethnicity, language and cultural politics in Indonesia and Malaysia.

Preface

Following a series of faculty seminars on globalization, organized by the Institute of Malaysian and International Studies (IKMAS) at the National University of Malaysia, and with support from the Pok Rafeah Foundation, the participants decided to write this book. The authors are all affiliated with IKMAS, and sought to bring their different disciplines – anthropology, economics, history, political science and sociology – to bear on a set of common research problems. Fourteen papers were presented at a workshop, held in Bangi, Malaysia, in April 1999, and made possible by generous funding from the Friedrich-Naumann-Stiftung and the assistance of the National University of Malaysia. The papers were discussed by fellow authors, other invited scholars, and members of civil society. Subsequently, an editorial committee selected eight of the papers for publication, contingent on revision and subject to final review.

Whereas the authors express different perspectives on, and advance diverse interpretations of, globalization, their contributions focus on a central research theme, elaborated in Chapter 1. Although this is not a book about Malaysia *per se*, all authors have carried out research there. Indeed, this book was written during the Asian economic crisis, which provided a backdrop for reviewing globalizing processes. This experience offers an important point of reference, though not an exclusive one, for the chapters that follow. It is important precisely because globalization studies are not really global. For the most part, globalization research has centred on the Organization for Economic Cooperation and Development countries, not the developing world. An objective of this book, then, is to begin to change the balance by posing a distinctive set of research questions and providing answers to them, if only in a preliminary manner, albeit one that deepens understanding about the nexus of globalization and development.

Abbreviations

APEC	Asia Pacific Economic Cooperation
APPA	Asia Pacific Peoples' Assembly
ASEAN	Association of Southeast Asian Nations
BRIMAS	Borneo Resource Institute
CEO	Chief Executive Officer
COLA	Cost of Living Allowance
EEC	European Economic Community
EPZ	Export-Processing Zone
FDI	Foreign Direct Investment
GDP	Gross Domestic Product
GFCF	Gross Fixed Capital Formation
GNP	Gross National Product
IKMAS	Institut Kajian Malaysia dan Antarabangsa (Institute of Malaysian and International Studies)
ILO	International Labour Organization
IMF	International Monetary Fund
IP	Indigenous People
ISA	Internal Security Act
KLSE	Kuala Lumpur Stock Exchange
MAI	Multilateral Agreement on Investment
MARA	Majlis Amanah Rakyat (People's Trust Council)
NGO	Non-Governmental Organization
NIE	Newly Industrialized Economy
NTT	Nippon Telegraph and Telephone Corporation
OECD	Organization for Economic Cooperation and Development
PCI	Per Capita Income
PNB	Permodalan Nasional Berhad (National Investment Corporation)

SIPA	Sarawak Indigenous People's Alliance
SUPP	Sarawak United People's Party
TNC	Transnational Corporation
TRIM	Trade-Related Investment Measures
UNCTAD	United Nations Conference on Trade and Development
WTO	World Trade Organization

Acknowledgements

An edited book, especially when undertaken with contributors resident on three continents and a publisher located in a fourth, requires considerable teamwork. Planned and coordinated by IKMAS, this volume would not have been possible without the support of the Friedrich-Naumann-Stiftung and its project officer Selena Gan, the Pok Rafeah Foundation, Universiti Kebangsaan Malaysia (the National University of Malaysia), and American University in Washington, DC. Special thanks are due to colleagues who participated in the April 1999 workshop whose selected papers, now much revised, appear in this volume. In addition to the contributing authors, they are Ahmat Adam, Askiah Adam, Asma Larif-Beatrix, Aziz Abdul Rahman, Barbara Leigh, Diana Wong, Khoo Kay Jin, Hishamuddin Rais, Linda Yarr, Mohd Hazim Shah, Mohd Yusof Kasim, Osman Rani Hassan, Rashila Ramli, Rüdiger Korff, Rosazman Hussin, Roslina Ismail, Rustam A. Sani, Saleha Hassan, Sharifah Zuriah Aljeffri, Syed Shahir, Wan Manan Wan Muda, and Victor Wee.

We also owe a debt of gratitude to our research assistants Athi Sivan Mariappan, an M.Phil. student at Universiti Kebangsaan Malaysia, and Aparna Devare and Robertus Imam, Ph.D. students at American University. IKMAS's general staff – Nor Hayati Sa'at, Roslina Rosli, Masrur Karsan, Umi Kalthum Meor Zainal Abidin, Zainon Khamis and Hasnul Hisham Zainal Abidin – contributed importantly to producing this book. Finally we are indebted to Shahid Qadir, the editor of *Third World Quarterly*, who brought out a special issue on 'Capturing Globalization' – Vol. 21, No. 6 (2000) – and kindly granted permission for the publication of its revised contents in this book.

1 Globalization
Captors and captives

James H. Mittelman

The act of capturing establishes a hierarchy between the captor and the captive. A hierarchy entails an ordering and a division of labour and power. The captors are of course on top, and the captured are at the bottom of the heap. Both within and between countries, there are many different shadings of this relationship. Thus, such structures must be contextualized and, today, are integral to an epochal transformation known as globalization.

More than a metaphor, the theme of capturing opens questions about large-scale historical change, and turns attention to some of the most vexing aspects of globalization: *control*, *autonomy* and *agency*. To what extent, and how, is the set of processes known as globalization being governed? If it is being governed, or if elements of it are subject to governance, then one would like to know whether there is effective management, what strategies are employed, and with what results. The tasks of control are both manifold and challenging in different arenas, i.e. at the global, regional, national and local levels. Moreover, there are the matters of defining the criteria of control, identifying who is doing the defining, and determining which interests are at stake.

In this introductory chapter, then, the objective is to formulate the core questions for analysis in the subsequent chapters. At bottom, they probe the interactions between globalization and the multiple actors, or combinations of them, who strive to dominate both its objective structures and the intersubjective processes that give it meaning. The challenge issued here is to consider these questions in light of Western scholarship and, going further, to decentre enquiry by drawing on varied non-Western discourses on religion, language and other spheres of social activity.

The problem in historical context

Whereas globalization has a long lineage, the last three decades of the twentieth century were a period of rapid structural change. In the 1970s, the international economy consisted of a handful of industrial countries that exported manufactured goods to a multitude of developing countries, which in turn sent abroad their primary products, mainly agricultural commodities and natural resources. Following the collapse of the Bretton Woods system of fixed exchange rates in 1971, a deep recession began in the United States in 1973, the year of the first oil shock, and ramified widely, initially in the West and then in the socialist and developing countries. After the Vietnam War, there was oversupply in primary commodity markets, and by the late 1970s, the hopes of a new international economic order, a package of proposals for international reform put forward by leaders from developing countries, were dashed. Marked by the simultaneous fall of commodity prices and the rise of real interest rates, the debt crisis of the early 1980s emerged. Although the United States was no longer the world's major creditor, but now its chief debtor, it maintained a position altogether different from that of developing countries whose balance of payments reflected deep structural problems. Against this backdrop, the pileup of large external debts allowed international creditors and donors to shape macroeconomic policy in many countries. Since the early 1980s, structural adjustment programmes mandated by international financial institutions further opened national economies and oriented, or reoriented, development strategies.

Meanwhile, deeply concerned about declining rates of productivity, the emphasis in the US economy changed from the old Fordist system of mass production, mass consumption towards post-Fordism, which allows for a higher degree of specialization, greater flexibility and faster turnover time. With the spread of the post-Fordist system, facilitated by new technologies, especially in transportation and communications, the 1980s witnessed a spatial reorganization of production. While the West and Japan largely moved from capital-intensive towards technologically intensive industries, some developing countries upgraded their manufacturing industries, initially through labour intensity, and climbed to a higher position in the global division of labour. This coincided with a changeover from import substitution policies to export promotion. Centring on greater integration in the global economy, the Reaganite–Thatcherite idea of neoliberalism extended from Anglo-America to other parts of the world, eroding barriers, relaxing restrictive frameworks for cross-border transactions, and allowing information, goods, and labour to flow more easily across national boundaries. Born in Anglo-America, neoliberalism is a culturally specific formula, one that has been extraordinarily mobile and propagated as a purportedly universal and moral proposition. But it has encountered other visions of the right and the good, such as a universal code of human rights and the notion of 'Asian values'.

After the Cold War, nonetheless, 'free markets', an idea and set of policies propounded and monitored by some states, public intellectuals, and international agencies, especially the International Monetary Fund (IMF), have became an icon as well as a matter of faith throughout much of the world. Foreign assistance, loans, credit ratings and foreign investment are conditioned on implementing neoliberal policies, namely deregulation, liberalization and privatization.

By the mid-1990s, there were signs of danger in emerging markets. In 1997–1998, financial turmoil, the meltdown of stock markets and in some cases (most notably, Indonesia) political turbulence struck parts of Asia. The contagion of economic decline threatened other locales: among them, and in different measure, South Africa, Brazil and Russia. At the turn of the millennium, what had been called 'the Asian crisis' escalated into a possible generator of global instability. Even if this crisis was a zigzag, not a complete breakdown, and notwithstanding substantial recovery in Asia, it is possible that periodic financial crises will be a regular feature of neoliberal globalization.

In the meantime, the power component in the new global configuration has triggered backlashes. At first, the impetus for resistance seemed to emanate from civil society, which began to scale up and thrust across borders. The ascendance of capital fragmented the identity of labour, and movements oriented to gender, the environment, religion, race and ethnicity asserted themselves singly or in combination. But backlashes against globalization appeared in other guises, including the groundswell of right-wing support for populist politicians, such as Pat Buchanan in the United States, Jean-Marie Le Pen in France, and Pauline Hanson of Australia. Conservatives in the US Congress and renowned neoliberal economists, such as Nobel laureate Milton Friedman and Jeffrey Sachs, expressed dismay over the workings of the market and the role of international financial institutions. While not opposing the market *per se*, some states, including France, resisted the Anglo-American version of neoliberal globalization, instead maintaining a large public sector and generous welfare provisions while only selectively deregulating and privatizing.

In another permutation, Malaysia, after widely opening its economy to foreign investors during its economic growth spurt, adopted selective and, as it turned out, temporary capital controls in 1998, restricting outflows of funds.

At issue in the uncertain period after the turn of the millennium are the struggles of a multiplicity of agents to subordinate the processes of globalization to their own desires and needs. In this contestation, markets are not only arenas of buyers and sellers, but also powerful forces increasingly detached from a bounded territory and with the capacity to discipline the state, evident in structural adjustment programmes, the ratings given by credit agencies such as Moody's and Standard and Poor's (which can make or break a developing economy), and attacks by currency speculators. Increasingly, markets are becoming dislodged from social and political control. Globally, there is no central source of order. No sovereign power can claim legitimate authority over the world market. Although national economies continue to serve as important arenas for markets, an upsurge of transnational flows challenges extant authority in this realm. What warrants investigation is not merely what states do to each other, the focus of realism, the dominant tradition in international relations. (Neorealists formulate the problematic of globalization by delimiting it as a matter of how the state adjusts its policies, without giving credence to the deep structural transformations under way in the global political economy. In this connection, see Waltz 1999: 693–700.) In fact, diverse contenders – both state and non-state actors – seek to capture political and economic power or aspects of it.

Capturing globalization is only partially a matter of state power. Not only may power be defined in terms of its overt and covert dimensions, but there is a structural sense of power at multiple levels, which involves both coercion and consent. It was Antonio Gramsci's insight that the mix of the two defines hegemony. From a Gramscian perspective, if consent is predominant over coercion, then a hegemonic constellation prevails. This is of course more cost effective than is the use of brute force, but the question, one that concerned classical writers such as Ibn Khaldun in the fourteenth century and Niccolo Machiavelli two centuries later, is how to use different capacities to ensure compliance and capture intersubjective under- standings. It will be recalled that in Machiavelli's view of the world as a thoroughly treacherous place, the qualities most useful to a prince, or that a prince should appear to have, are likened to those of a centaur: half-man, half-beast. Both require a capacity to know how to employ them:

Thus, you must know that there are two kinds of combat: one with laws, the other with force. The first is proper to man, the second to beasts; but because the first is often not enough, one must have recourse to the second.

(Machiavelli 1985: 69)

This is very much a matter of determining what are the positions of authority and which prince – collective agency writ large – will hold them.

In a globalizing world, the lines of legitimate authority are blurred. This tendency is especially apparent with regard to licit and illicit activities. As in Russia, states are sometimes in league with organized crime, and criminal activities, such as drug trafficking, are becoming globalized. In this and other 'spheres of authority' (a concept borrowed from Rosenau 1997: 39–41), *there is no dichotomy between the captor and the captive*. Novel, complex hierarchical relationships have formed, are fluid, and may overlap. Moreover, global hierarchies are manifest within regions, but refract differently from one region to another, and crucial intraregional differences are apparent.

Objectives

To examine these hierarchies, a preliminary task is to identify the globalizers, to determine who are the sponsors and torchbearers of globalizing processes. Conversely, one must know who is harmed by – who bears the pain of – this parametric transformation. The contributing authors will probe the interactions among the actors. In addition, lurking behind the identities of these agents lies the issue of their interests in the overall configuration of power relations. This points to the question of control: who or what are the arbiters of order? While indicating the array of actors engaged in globalization processes, consideration is, above all, given to the ways that they are attempting to capture, i.e. direct or redirect, changing global structures, and whether they are doing so in a democratic or undemocratic manner. Posing these questions underlines the importance and urgency of thinking concretely about agency without being unduly voluntarist about large-scale structural change.

Working amid the salutary *and* sordid effects of market-based integration, the contributors have gained perspective on the trade-offs – the opportunities and constraints – in the globalization matrix. The trauma associated with environmental abuses that deeply affect daily life in many countries, large fluctuations in the value of national currencies, and the loss of confidence in some economies have animated searching enquiry into underlying causes, both regionally and at a global level.

Thus, the main objective in this book is to explain how different communities try to capture social and political control of the dynamics of globalization, specifically as they interpenetrate conditions in Southeast Asia and also on an interregional basis. Whereas many researchers in this field have rightly focused on big, abstract structures, it is also important to provide detailed description of globalization as a contested process. The outcome of this contestation is in no way predetermined but open ended. Furthermore, the playing field is not level; it is tilted in various directions, and firm rules are lacking. If so, one must shift attention to the ways that agents seek to maintain or undermine global structures. In the globalization literature, theories and concepts have largely travelled from the West to other parts of the world. Indeed, globalization studies are not really global but primarily emanate from Western intellectual traditions and practice. While considering the extant literature, the authors contributing to this volume will also draw on non-Western discourses. Whereas this analysis does not purport to offer a fully fledged alternative framework for studying globalization, it does bring to bear the experience of diverse scholars who have carried out extensive research on non-Western encounters with globalization, and points to new directions deemed worthy of pursuing.

This undertaking is necessarily interdisciplinary. One of the most promising features of globalization research is that it helps to overcome the compartmentalization of knowledge and calls for a holistic approach. Time has been the province of historians; space, the *métier* of geographers. Now, the disciplines of history and geography are central to understanding world order, and political economy also requires the expertise of sociology and anthropology. To be sure, the cultural aspects of globalization involve practices and representations, matters long treated in the humanistic sciences. Globalization studies thus bridge diverse fields of investigation.

The contributors to this volume are drawn from the disciplines of anthropology, economics, history, political science, and sociology. While they adopt different perspectives, let me offer a point of departure, a frame of reference that others can use as a target in their own chapters. There is a line of thinking that regards globalization as a compression of time and space (Giddens 1990; Harvey 1990; Robertson 1992). That is, with new technologies that speed transactions and shrink distances, both time barriers and spatial constraints are lessened. Anthony Giddens sees this process as part of the inherent unfolding of modernity and as a spur toward interconnectedness. Elaborating on the concept of time–space compression, David Harvey shows the radically different ways that thinking about, and the representations of, the ordering of time and space have changed. Both Harvey and Roland Robertson regard time–space compression as a cultural force, and for Robertson, it is driven by global consciousness. Importantly, one must look at the links between this compression and social relations, for globalizing processes are not socially or politically neutral. Rather, they are both constitutive of and constitute social relations. Of course, the argument mounted by these theorists becomes entangled with the debates over modernity and the postmodern critique. In my view, it is useful to separate analysis of globalization from any notion that it is necessarily an outcome of a process such as modernity, as if it had its own laws. To think otherwise runs the risk of positing an end-point, a teleology (Albrow 1996: 99). Rather, if globalization is a contested and political phenomenon, then it cannot have a predetermined outcome. A political agenda of inevitability overlooks the fact that globalization was made by humans, and, if so, can be unmade or remade by humankind.

Also, if globalization theories offer the advantage of seeing the parts from the view of the whole, and if the whole global political economy has its own dynamics, then the parts are subject to systemic effects. However, what bears emphasis is that the system affects the components in very different ways. Globalization is a partial, not a totalizing, phenomenon. Countries and regions are tethered to some aspects of globalization, but sizeable pockets remain removed from it. Globalization contains a dialectic of inclusion and exclusion.

It is worth emphasizing that globalization is not a single, unified process but a set of interactions that may be best approached from different observation points. First, it may be seen as a complex of historical processes. The trajectories differ in various regions of the world, though all are directly or indirectly tied to the central institutions and growth mechanisms of the world economy. Second, globalization may be understood as material processes closely related to the accumulation of capital. It is caught up with the innovations in capitalism, especially the inner workings of competition, pressures that may be called hypercompetition. Third, globalization may be regarded as an ideology – the neoliberal belief in free markets and faith in the beneficial role of competition (Mittelman 1996a). Hence, globalization is an extensive set of interactions, dialectically integrating and disintegrating economies, polities, and societies around the world. Capital is in ascendance, while labour and nationality – the two major identities of the twentieth century – are fragmented into multiple identifiers, including gender, religion, race, and ethnicity. Furthermore, the globalization trend offers gains in productivity, technological advances, higher living standards, more jobs, broader access to consumer products at lower cost, widespread dissemination of information and knowledge, reductions in poverty in some parts of the world, and a release from traditional social hierarchies in many countries. Yet there is a dark side to globalization: the integration of markets threatens tightly knit communities and sources of solidarity, dilutes local cultures, and portends a loss of control, particularly in very poor countries. This massive socio-historical transformation warrants empirical and theoretical exploration of its underlying dynamics.

Research questions

The editors of this book have posed four research questions, though others could be added. The following questions provide a framework of considerations for critical scrutiny by the contributors, each of whom has been asked to respond to some or all of these issues.

1 *Globalization is rapidly reorganizing people's livelihood and modes of social existence, but without systematic reflection on the values that undergird this set of processes. What are these moral codes? Whose ethics are dominant? What are the results of attempts to balance divergent norms such as the commitment to sustained economic growth and equity?*

The first question, or bundle of questions, suggests that globalization is not merely an economic process, or, to put it differently, that markets are social institutions encoded with normative claims. In fact, the ethics of globalization are understudied and have been poorly grasped in the social sciences. Clearly, there are values associated with neoliberal globalization – efficiency, competitiveness, profitability, and individualism – that form a normative paradigm based on instrumental rationality, and may be seen as part of a larger attempt to assert universal truths.

The key to the argument about universals is that through ideas, humans have access to truths, a universe that transcends time and space. In this universe, knowledge is supposed to be generated without recourse to observation. The logic is used in the realm of numbers (mathematics), beauty as well as the good (philosophy), and the spirit (religion). Measures of goodness, it is held, can be related to this world, the here-and-now, through the ideals of universal rights and universal principles. When employed in public policy, these are made use of in science and the logic of rational choice in such realms as environmental economics (Yearley 1996: 17–23, 125).

Ultimately, the application of putative universal discourses becomes caught up with power relations, and also may result in lapses in critical discussion about ethics. Consider the period of economic ascendancy in Eastern Asia in the 1980s and early 1990s. The adoption of free-market principles led to claims that the 'miracle' of rapid economic growth was related to something different about the way that Asians organize their societies, markets, and states. Various commentators praised the high savings rates, job security, low-cost housing for workers, emphasis on education, and religious traditions that stress consensus. Whereas some observers trumpeted the virtues of 'Asian values', others celebrated the alleged fusion of the best practices and values from Asian and Western civilizations. However, when the economic crisis jolted Asia in 1997, attention turned to the underside of these same values, namely crony capitalism, corruption, and secrecy – problems that surely are not unique to any region. In Asia, there were immediate calls for bailouts and other rescue packages, redoubling the involvement of international financial institutions in the region.

The World Bank and the IMF play a direct role in the drive to universalize the values of neoliberal globalization. Responding to debt crises, the Bretton Woods institutions assist donor countries within a framework that safeguards the international monetary system. Their assistance is predicated on the obligation by borrowing countries to meet repayments by increasing export earnings, attracting foreign investment, decreasing government spending, and diminishing social policy in areas such as health care and education. There is considerable controversy over whether this formula alleviates or hampers distressed economies, and over how the burden is distributed. An ethical dilemma is apparent in the types of balances struck between the rise in environmental harm and the drop in expenditure on environmental management. In this sphere, hard neoclassical logic brings to light the clash between economic reform and equity. The political decision to emphasize economic globalization coincides, and seems to collide, with the diminished capacity of the state to protect, or indifference towards, the most marginalized zones of the global political economy and the poor in other regions.

With the restructuring of the state, the local level – associations within civil society such as families and religious institutions – is generally deemed to be most directly involved in ethical development. Indeed, the agents of socialization are most effective in terms of early childhood experiences, when they shape affective orientation, the basis for later cognitive learning. At first blush, it may appear that the globalization scenario is remote from this stage of human development. New technologies in the computer industry, worldwide finance, cross-border mergers, transnational corporations, changes in production structures, and institutions such as the IMF and the World Trade Organization all seem removed from what goes on day to day in the household. But are they? If both husband and wife are compelled to join the workforce, if a new production system dramatically alters who is at home and who provides childcare, if the media broadcast new norms directly into the living room, if toys and clothing, not to mention food, reflect the consumer tastes of other cultures, it would appear that the impact of globalization, including its big structures and heavy processes, on ethics in the earliest years is a matter that must be subject to close scrutiny. If so, the effects of globalization on ethics may then be weighed in terms of political accountability, the incidence of poverty, and social welfare policy.

Yet it is also important to consider whether globalization opens space for ethical development, especially in regard to influences that emanate beyond the nation-state. The spread of norms across borders takes place through macroregionalism (e.g. the forum for Asia Pacific Economic Cooperation) and subregionalism (e.g. the Association of Southeast Asian Nations, 'growth triangles', and 'growth polygons') as well as from the elaboration of international law as it adapts to new conditions (e.g. the globalization of organized crime). In the areas of human rights, environmental policy, and gender, groups within civil society are advocating that ethical standards be advanced, monitored, and safeguarded. These groups appeal not only to moral sensibilities within the state, but also to putative universal norms. Globalization is, in fact, establishing new openings for non-state actors – what Sassen (1998: 94) calls 'new sites of normativity' – pressuring the state, transgressing the authority of the state over its citizens, and thereby eroding the boundaries of jurisdiction defined by the Westphalian interstate system. In light of these considerations, one of the challenges facing the contributing authors is to assess the balances between economic globalization and social justice.

> 2   *Inasmuch as communities at various levels are not mere objects of, but agents in, the globalization scenario, how do they optimize their positions vis-à-vis the currents of globalization and attempt to use this trend for their advantage?*

If globalization is not a universal that can be analysed regardless of time and place, then interests must be recognized and brought into the analysis. The play of interest is one factor that sparks off the politics of identity. To the extent that globalization entails a restructuring at several levels, there are new winners and losers: neoliberal values and policies are not neutral in terms of social relations, but set conditions for the interactions between captors and the captive. Hence, along with the values in the globalization paradigm, the identities of these groups and subgroups – identities based on class, gender, religion, race, and ethnicity – must be delimited. Although there is not a sharp bifurcation between the captors and the captive, but an array of agents in the hierarchy of globalization, captors and captives are still important markers for trying to determine exactly who are the globalizers, and how do they benefit? Conversely, who is harmed by globalization, and how do these groups react?

To navigate the currents of globalization, various actors develop strategies, by which I mean the actual ways that people, whose modes of existence are altered by new structures (e.g. through job loss, encroachment on community lands, or threats to cultural integrity), respond in a sustained manner towards achieving certain objectives. At one level, there is the question of how is the state managing globalization through its policies in the realms of technology, manufacturing, trade, human resource development, and so on? Clearly, there are major differences in the strategies adopted by states in close proximity to one another within hierarchical and both global and regional divisions of labour and power. Cognizant of state policies, firms, of course, must also seek to position themselves strategically so as to capitalize on the opportunities of globalization. Although there is no unified strategy, like other actors, corporations have to adjust to the changing parameters within which they operate.

Innovative strategies specifically crafted to capture globalization, or aspects of it, are not merely stabs in the dark at an amorphous phenomenon. In civil society, some – by no means all – groups that are self-organizing have engaged in self-conscious strategizing about how best to respond to globalizing processes. While forms of struggle differ, groups adopt varied means to contest, scale up or down, and link objectively and/or subjectively to their counterparts in other countries or regions. With sustained access to communication technologies that construct and maintain communities of like-minded individuals, local movements may become transnational or global, i.e. networks of activists that coordinate their endeavours in an attempt to harness or at least mitigate the deleterious effects of the market (Mittelman 2000: 179–222).

---

3   *In so far as globalization is a multilevel phenomenon, what are the foremost cultural and political attempts in different contexts to govern the market? With what results?*

Many studies (e.g. Dicken 1998) centre primarily, though not exclusively, on the geoeconomic dimensions of globalization because of the centrality of markets. In this literature (e.g. Strange 1998), a great deal of attention is given to production, finance, and trade. At the same time, some globalization researchers are wary of an imbalance, with emphasis on economics and technology at the expense of cultural and political globalization. Indeed, if globalization is not a single but a multilevel phenomenon, one research strategy is to employ a holistic approach and turn to cultural political economy.

Whereas hypercompetition may be a causal element in the rise of globalization, it is caught up with cultural structures. Just as globalization fosters large structures in the economy (e.g. megamergers) and the polity (e.g. macroregions such as the European Union), it also fragments cultures. Large markets and the diffusion of new norms erode cultures, in some instances fostering particularities and contributing to the formation of multiple identities. Hence, the fault line in Canada, surely a precarious entity, is between the Anglophones and Francophones, but within Quebec, Ontario, British Columbia, and other parts of this huge expanse, numerous minorities, including very different Amerindian groups, the Acadians in New Brunswick, and Inuits in the Northwest Territories, Nunavut, and northern Quebec, have clamoured for their own 'rights'. This persistent debate is about language, region, race, and ethnicity. Additionally, the politics of collective identity in Canada also touches on redrawing the boundaries of a country (in one scenario, with English Canada joining the United States) and transforming the political landscape. This emotionally charged issue poses a deeper question: in the context of globalization, when the basic units in which peoples have organized themselves since the Treaty of Westphalia in 1648 are increasingly porous and penetrated from without, what is the meaning of 'nation', 'country', 'state', and, by extension, 'citizen'? Are there altered meanings, and do the meanings differ in the part of the world that invented the Westphalian system and in the postcolonial regions onto which this system was grafted?

To get at these questions, one must grasp the ways in which culture becomes an ordering force in globalization. What is required is to understand how culture frames meaning so that people form their convictions, establish a sense of themselves, and maintain their solidarities (Geertz 1998). Cultural globalization operates both as a top-down process, which is promoted by cultural industries (various forms of entertainment, films, television), and as a bottom-up response to these powerful structures. In fledgling form, a new politics is emerging, which manifests as a cultural riposte. Increasingly apparent, to varying degrees in different places, is the rise of non-state politics. While the state remains an important arena, in some cases contesting aspects of the neoliberal matrix (e.g. France) and in other cases accommodating it (especially the poorest countries, where an acute loss of control is endemic), non-state politics is becoming a more salient venue for devising solutions to problems and fashioning alternatives. Inasmuch as disgruntlement with the state regardless of which party holds power is a widespread phenomenon, reflected in low voter turnout in some countries and indicated in survey research, people are turning to a practical politics of another sort: voting with their feet by migrating to a different locale, participating in the parallel market (often across the border), and engaging in ethnic politics through family networks which, in the case of the Chinese diaspora (among others), form a transnational division of labour and capital. There is a multiplicity and divergence of historically contingent ways in which people respond to the tensions generated by globalizing structures.

---

4 *Are there internal tensions among the processes subsumed under globalization? What are the social limits to a framework based on neoliberal values and policies?*

Explicit in the discussion heretofore is that globalization involves a series of interactions among the economic, political, and cultural spheres of life. It also appears in diverse sizes and shapes in different regions. When globalizing structures meet local conditions, myriad combinations are formed. True, in certain respects, global capitalism is a national phenomenon, but national political economies are in very different positions, some more or less open, dynamic, and vulnerable to captivity than are others. Indeed, it is important to note the distinctive ways in which capitalism is organized in various regions and countries today; however, the proposition that globalizing forces promote diversity, not homogeneity, does not invalidate the globalization scenario. Rather, by historicizing the construct, researchers help to refine it.

Inasmuch as globalization is not a uniform structure, one must attempt to interrelate multiple levels of analysis. I will turn briefly to two sets of interactions: politics and economics, and economics and culture (points elaborated in Mittelman 2000: especially chap. 12).

The first tension surrounds the issue of accountability. The easing of borders as a result of deregulation and the consequent surge of capital flows from other economies, large-scale transfers of population from some parts of the world to others, the increase in mergers and mega-acquisitions, instantaneous movements of finance through electronic space, and growing concentrations of capital are all part of the trend whereby the economy becomes disembedded from society, a pattern noted by Karl Polanyi over fifty years ago (Polanyi 1957, originally published 1944). Flows of capital and labour take place at a horizontal level within the world economy and are only partially susceptible to control by sovereign units. Politically, the globe is organized into vertical compartments that attempt to capture these transactions. State institutions with territorial scope, such as central banks, are unable to exercise extraterritorial authority – say, over the foreign currency market, now a business worth 1.5 trillion dollars a day. State-sanctioned agencies supposed to hold a legitimate monopoly to enforce compliance over their own domain appear to be stymied by increasing deterritorialization in matters of economic governance. Meanwhile, with globalization, pro-democracy forces in many parts of the world are pressing their political leaders for greater account-ability within the nation-state, but accountability in the global economy is elusive and thus far exceeds the grasp of these forces.

Like pro-democracy forces, other advocacy groups – varied social movements – are also trying to open political space. Just as some of them want to build larger solidarities across borders, other groups, often those most threatened by globalizing trends, are atavistic and seek to preserve, or imagine, local and particularistic identities, as is the case with right-wing militias in the United States and anti-immi-grant groups from Scandinavia to South Africa. Whereas some wings of civil society attempt to capture parts of the mega phenomenon known as globalization, others are actually sponsored by its purveyors (large corporations, international financial institutions, state-run bilateral agencies, etc.) or even hold pivotal positions of state power, as in the Philippines and South Africa today, which perhaps is one form of capturing globalization inasmuch as a depen-dent state is tied to social forces partly rooted outside the national domain. However, this in turn raises both tactical and ethical dilemmas about the proper role of civil society and whether it is being coopted and becoming corrupt. Certainly, civil society is riddled with internal tensions.

Civil society has became an important element in globalization precisely because of a tension between a deterritorialized economy and national culture. Commanding new technologies, the entertain-ment industry, led by US firms, is beaming programmes and films onto screens around the world. Accompanying the movies, serials, sporting events, and newscasts are distinct values such as individu-alism and consumerism. Of course, other industries are hard at work, and draw immigrants to overseas operations, exposing them to new values, which are later transported back to their home countries when the returnees visit there or resettle. Both the entertainment industry and the labour market are modalities whereby a globalizing economy undercuts national and local life-ways, in some cases helping to ease indigenous forms of social control (e.g. patriarchy), but often at the expense of cultural dignity.

Embracing a neoliberal framework of liberalization, deregulation, and privatization, the globalization paradigm clearly offers benefits to all who would partake in this process, but in an uneven manner. The higher the level of globalization, the greater the degree of marginalization. Put differently, there are rips and tears in the fabric of globalization. Enclaves of poverty within the wealthy countries and a multitude of impoverished countries, except for their upper strata – most apparent in, but not unique to, Africa – fall into the breach. At the same time, the neoliberal formula prescribes delinking economic reform from social policy, which places a greater burden on women, the primary care givers and users of health facilities. By all indications, globalization and marginalization are two sides of the same coin. If so, one must consider: is globalization ethically sustainable?

Preview

The preceding discussion has provided a brief view of the issues, concepts, and considerations that guide the chapters in this book. The four questions posed for the contributors to explore are what binds the individual chapters. In addition, I have formulated specific questions within these questions.

The book is organized around four aspects of globalization, and responses to the research questions framed above are threaded through these clusters of chapters. Following this introduction and that by Clive Kessler, who offers a broad comparative and historical overview of the norms inscribed in globalization, are two chapters on market forces: Rajah Rasiah examines private capital flows across borders, and Ishak Shari probes poverty-generating structures. Then Sabihah Osman explores the ways in which political life are being redefined under globalization: the changing role of the state and democratization, with reference to the indigenous people of Sarawak, Malaysia. Finally, attention turns to the socio-cultural dimensions of globalization – Abdul Rahman Embong on the nexus of transnational class relations and globalization, and Sumit Mandal regarding cultural disruptions in culture and new patterns – before Norani Othman and Clive Kessler present conclusions about the extent to which any group, or which groups, are capturing globalization and the riposte from those held captive.

2 Globalization

Another false universalism?

Clive S. Kessler

> The only philosophy which can be responsibly practised in the face of despair is the attempt to contemplate all things as they would present themselves from the standpoint of redemption.
>
> (Adorno 1974: 247)

This discussion poses a central and fateful question: whether globalization represents just another – and merely the most recent – of the false or compromised universalisms which have emerged within human history and been offered as providing the key to its immanent logic, its irresistible trajectory. The answer to be offered – 'perhaps, but perhaps not' – may seem unsurprising and even unsatisfactory. But what matters at the outset is not the question's answer but its meaning: what does the idea of a false or compromised universalism suggest and why does it matter? Clarifying these issues involves a serious analytical engagement with a question with which many popular and facile theories of globalization – all the unexamined rhetoric of a 'borderless world' and the 'global village' – merely play: the gradual emergence in our time (or just over our temporal horizon) of a comprehensive and inclusive human interdependence, and its effect upon the human moral imagination.

Globalization: modernist and postmodernist accounts

J.K. Galbraith (1998: 26) has remarked that he can accept pretty much everything about globalization except the name. The processes he sees as mundane, the label given collectively to them unhelpful. Some of us feel a different ambivalence: not the label given to various globalization processes, bringing them together as a single phenomenon, but the various theories advanced to characterize and explain those processes are what seems most problematic. These theories appear not so much wrong as insufficient.

Over recent years a vast scholarly literature has built up on the subject of globalization. Countless academics in the social sciences, working under the ever more exigent imperatives of the political economy of career survival and advancement in universities across the world, have produced literally hundreds of books and thousands of articles probing the question of globalization. In this sense the globalization debate is itself a major global phenomenon, a key instance of the very issue it seeks to explore.[1] To contribute further, to offer yet another small piece, to the already gross body of this scholarly monster is not hard; to make sense of the now monumental globalization literature is a problem. But addressing this problem, in a brief caricature perhaps, is a necessary preliminary to understanding what is humanly at stake in globalization and its discourses.

For all its plenitude of analysis and commentary, the vast literature about globalization seems to fall into two main parts. These might be characterized as the modernist and postmodernist paradigms of globalization theory. The first focuses on the emergence and consolidation of a single world economy; it devotes itself to probing and explaining the political economy, and sometimes also the attendant sociology, of an intensifying human interdependence. It comes in two forms: its liberal version sees that emerging interdependence as unifying, benign and equalizing, its radical or sceptical version as preserving old and even creating new forms of social inequality, hierarchy and exclusion.

The second approach surveys, often with uncritical satisfaction, the emergence through technical innovation of a single human community: a virtual community, perhaps an incipient community-in-the-making, whose members have become complexly involved in one another's lives, if only as prospective auditors and spectators, through the development of the so-called new information and communications technologies. Its proponents see a world not divided into differing time zones by the rising and setting of the sun along the various meridians of longitude (or by any other major lines of structural cleavage) but a single human network of instantaneous 'real-time' interaction; for them, the way in and the speed with which money can be transferred around the world (by those, of course, who have access to it and oversee its movements) provide the exemplar of all human interaction and communication generally. Concerned less with political economy than with communications and the new information technologies (as if CNN and AOL and the Internet existed outside of the realm of commodities and massive corporate interests), this approach is often found and is especially favoured within the new field of 'cultural studies' (while the first approach is still based, but does not stand uncontested by insurgent proponents of the new 'communications paradigm', in the established disciplinary fields of sociology, political science and international relations).

Transcending their opposition, an apparent reconciliation or at least combination of these two main approaches is to be found in the theories of those such as Anthony Giddens who speak of the compression of time and space differences as fundamental to the contemporary human condition.[2] These hybrid theories seek to graft the insights of the postmodernist communications theorists onto the basic political economy framework of established disciplinary analysis. In the case of Giddens, he has sought not simply to argue this approach intellectually but actually to demonstrate it performatively in his five 1999 BBC Reith Lectures, offered from four different locations across the globe and backed up by a website where listeners worldwide could engage in debate with him, and one another, over the meaning and implications of globalization processes.

Much of the vast literature on globalization, and of the debate about its meaning and implications, falls within these two, or perhaps three, main paradigms. Together, they tell us a lot, but not everything. To question their exhaustiveness and seek to go beyond them is to argue that, separately and together, they are not so much wrong as insufficient – that they leave unaddressed some important issues which are fundamental to understanding the significance of the globalization processes now intensifying within and transforming the social worlds in which we live.

To identify these further issues, it is necessary to recognize that globalization, as a key feature of contemporary social life, does not simply work its way upon important practical dimensions (economic, political, communicative) of contemporary life but, in doing so, involves a central philosophical issue. What the increasing, and increasingly manifest, human interdependence that modern globalization processes promote, and highlight in an entirely new perspective, is the question of humankind – the moral issue of human equality and universalism – itself. Historically, this issue has already surfaced in several forms in humankind's gradually evolving self-understanding, but in quite problematic and compromised ways; whether the way in which it is now posed by the rapid advance of globalization processes is any less problematic remains to be seen.

First intuitions of human universality

A central and perennial problem facing humankind is the question of its own nature. Partly, this involves the question of the relations of humans to the rest of creation around them, in all its diversity; from the exploration of this puzzle the modern natural sciences have arisen. Another key part, the one that concerns us here, is the question of humankind's relations with itself, in all its own complex internal diversity. From grappling with this second puzzle the philosophical imagination and the modern social sciences have emerged.

The central conundrum here is that if humankind is so diverse, is it and how can it be one; and if it is one, how is its diversity to be understood and explained? How can one simultaneously recognize and talk about both the unity and the diversity of humankind; in what intellectual terms and moral language is this possible? Throughout much of human history, the diversity of humankind has been obvious to most of its members, obvious to their immediate senses as they have encountered and seen and heard speaking people from neighbouring villages and far-off lands. What has not been obvious to their senses has been the fact of human unity – and the fact of human moral equality and the universality of the human condition – which the fact of the unity of humankind implies.

Yet despite its abstract difficulty, throughout their history humans have in various forms glimpsed this intellectual problem and its solution, but always in partial or what eventually proved to be limited or even compromised forms. The first of these recognitions or intimations was in the universalistic religions, especially in the Abrahamic faith communities of Judaism, Christianity and Islam. These provided the first explicit and elaborated articulations of the view that, even if they were not or did not appear equal and alike among themselves on earth in their own understandings of themselves and one another, there was a God in Heaven who was the Creator of all human beings and who was the author of a single moral law that applied to all of them by virtue of their common humanity: a universal moral law to which all were subject and which all were obliged and equally bound to uphold. In this sense, whatever their inequalities on earth, humans, being equally subject to the divine law and requirements of their Creator, were under the divine dispensation – from God's own standpoint – equal among themselves.[3]

The monotheistic religious conscience has often had to live, in the historical civilizations which it has founded, with a painful and often unresolved tension between the fact of human social inequality and an awareness of the religiously inspired moral imperative of human unity and universality. Yet despite these tensions and imperfections, the idea of the moral equality of human beings, of the unity of humankind and of the underlying universality of the human condition first made its appearance in the world, in human consciousness, in this religious form or idiom. It was impelled not directly by any process of mutual recognition between different types of human beings but indirectly, by the acknowledgement among different kinds of human beings of their subordination to a single God of all humankind. The moral unity of humankind, that is, was not an obvious or irresistible conclusion, drawn by the evidence of the senses from actual encounters between diverse human beings, but an abstract implication which flowed from acknowledging that there was some standpoint outside of humanity itself from which humankind appeared as one, despite its own spectacular internal diversity. The idea of a God in Heaven with a single moral law to which all humankind was subject provided such an external and superior point of reference from which humans could imagine they might themselves be seen, a hypothetical or conceivable standpoint for catching moral sight of humanity's ontological commonality.

Yet this idea of the unity of humankind and of the equality of all human beings followed only as an implication, not as evidence of the human senses themselves. Not all humans were sensitive to this implication of their underlying unity and commonality; and among those who were, it emerged not as an empirically based conclusion but as a moral intuition. That the idea of the unity of humankind and the commonality of the human condition emerged as a moral intuition or inference was, however, characteristic not only of this first form of its recognition but in subsequent forms as well. What makes the present historical moment, in an era of accelerating globalization, distinctive is that the basis for such a recognition is now becoming objectively grounded, materially and socially. The idea itself is now ceasing to be a problematic moral intuition and, at least potentially, is becoming grounded empirically and existentially. But to say that now is to leap ahead of the analysis.

While it emerged within the monotheistic religious imagination, the historical fate of this powerful idea of the unity of humankind was to remain unrealized under religious sponsorship. In its Jewish version, it became closely implicated with what was to become a small and distinctive community committed to sustaining on the margins of ancient and more modern history the idea of its own civilizational mission and particularity.[4] In Christianity it was tied in with the civilizational career of an expanding power that pursued world domination and, at its imperial heights, even invoked its religious faith to cultivate a scorn for the 'lesser breeds' of humankind: those who lacked advanced technology and the related ability to sustain their political independence were seen by ascendant Christendom and then post-Christian Europe as lesser kinds of human beings or even less than human beings. Even in Islam, which articulated at the level of principle the most inclusive version of this morally universalistic faith, the realization of a truly inclusive moral universalism based upon the recognition of the unity of all humankind was thwarted. In the case of Islam it was precluded both by the absoluteness of its own doctrinal dichotomization – born of Islamic civilization's spectacular growth and successful political expansion during its early centuries – of the 'faithful' and the 'infidel'; and thereafter by the historical vicissitudes faced by the Islamic world, especially in its centuries-long antagonistic civilizational encounter with the world of militant Christendom and its post-Christian Western successors, from the times of the Crusades to the so-called late twentieth-century 'clash of civilizations'.[5]

Human universalism: compromised intimations

It was the fate of the Abrahamic faiths – with their core idea of a single God and moral law to which all humankind was bound – to sponsor but, for historical reasons, not actually to achieve or realize the sublime moral vision which faith implied of the unity of humankind, the moral equality of all human beings and the commonality or universality of the human condition. But this fate was not to be theirs alone. Other intellectual constructs and edifices centring elsewhere than on the One God subsequently emerged in the historical advance of human self-understanding which also met with the same fate, collapsing before the same limitation of partiality. Again, the underlying implication of the unity of humankind from the standpoint or perspective of some entity or principle apparently outside and apart from real living humans capitulated in the same way, and worse, to historical circumstances. In all cases, the key moral implication of human unity and equality which was entailed by the dominant intellectual construct and even briefly emerged from within it became articulated in a less than universal, and hence in a morally compromised, form. In each case the universalism promoted was a compromised or false universalism.

Of these compromised intuitions of human universalism three deserve brief mention. The first was the classical liberal theory of the state, in which the sovereign authority of the state structure itself took over God's place as the impersonal, impartial and external force or entity from whose perspective or standpoint all individuals were equal, identical in formal rights and substitutable for one another in their different identities. Here the idea of the 'abstract individual' – equally applicable to all living individuals, transcending their differences, in which all actual individuals were to see their own essential features and against which they were to measure themselves – was again fashioned, emerging this time not as 'the believer' but 'the subject' or 'citizen'. But as a number of critics of the liberal state have argued, from Marx in his critique of Hegel (1975 and, in more elaborated form, 1970b) to modern feminist critiques (e.g. Pateman 1989) of the covertly gendered character of the liberal notion of the citizen as masculine, the state routinely and even necessarily fails to achieve the imperfect universalism which it problematically articulates; in fact, the liberal state succeeds best in doing its murky job, some argue, precisely by its success in masquerading as the embodiment of a moral and human universalism which it in fact belies, manipulates and negates. Moral universalism appears under the aegis of the modern liberal state and its theory in an imperfect, corrupted, even bastardized form.

The same criticism can be made of modern economic theory. It pursues the identical strategy and is based on precisely the same intellectual foundation, except that it has replaced God as the external standpoint and impersonal measure against which all individuals are to be humanly and morally evaluated not with the state but with the market and its 'sacred' principles (and the 'believer' or the successor 'subject/citizen' with that calculating and transacting and maximizer, *homo economicus*). Clearly, a considerable part of the attraction of so-called 'market fundamentalism' or 'economic rationalism'[6] has been its peculiarly moral appeal to those who have provided the electoral weight for its political successes: to those who respond to its canonization of abstract individualism not intellectually but almost viscerally – to its core inner implication of, and its widely articulated adherence to, the principle of 'no favouritism' for 'special interests' but rather 'formally equal treatment' by the market, and by a state apparatus committed to the supremacy of market principles, for all individuals regardless of their various identifying and differentiating particularities. Some, of course, support such policies because they see through the intellectual shadow-play and see that such policies favour certain established interests, including their own; but many more (one is tempted to think) support such policies quite 'uncritically', not looking behind the ideological play of alluring universalisms but responding directly, if often out of complex *ressentiment*, to their symbolic and emotional power.[7]

The fact that such people may often be acting against their own interests in responding to such appeals and supporting socially destructive policies only demonstrates the enormous resonant power of an idiom of moral universalism and its implied notions of formal human equality. Not recognizing the fact that, like the law (as Anatole France (1924: 91) memorably remarked), the market 'in its majestic impartiality forbids rich and poor alike to sleep under bridges, to beg in the streets and to steal bread', these ardent electoral supporters of parties promoting the supremacy of market principles and market-driven policies provide proof both of the strength of appeals to moral universalism and of the compromised, distorted and even corrupted form in which human universalism appears under the aegis and within the intellectual constructs of modern economics.

A third and far more honourable endeavour to fathom and articulate the notion of the unity of humankind, the moral equality of all human beings and the commonality of the human situation is that which has been provided by the modern social sciences, especially anthropology which in this regard epitomizes their common quest. Anthropology poses as its central project the detailed, grounded, empirical and complexly circumstantial investigation of the central philosophical question of what it means to be human. With its concept of 'culture' and its appreciation of the diversity of 'cultures', anthropology not only sought but actually succeeded in devising a set of intellectual terms in which it was simultaneously possible to contemplate both the unity and the diversity of humankind – not as some sort of intriguing paradox but as two aspects of the one reality, two sides of the same coin.

What modern anthropology, especially of the Boasian lineage, succeeded in providing was an understanding that there is something generic about being human which all humans by definition share, but that this common generic humanity is a set of potentialities which must always be realized in particular individuals in particular ways, in the context of their time and place and society. Everyone has within them what is generically human, anthropology contends, but all are required by the incomplete and open-ended nature of human nature itself to realize that generic capacity – the possibility and also the necessity for cultural elaboration and expression of biological nature – in a specific way and form. One cannot become, on the basis of that general human capacity and potentiality, a human being in general; one can only and must become a specific human being, defined and shaped by the historical circumstances of a particular society, of a particular time and place.[8]

Not simply as an aspiration but in a intellectually coherent and grounded and therefore persuasive fashion, Boasian anthropology yielded a non-essentialist notion of human ontology: one that acknowledged diversity and promoted pluralism rather than presuming and entrenching uniformitarianism. This was a truly moral and progressive insight, as well as a great intellectual advance on the purely speculative accounts of the human situation which had hitherto been the best that humanity could provide of its own ontology and existential situation. In its own internal intellectual terms, modern anthropology largely solved the moral and philosophical question of the nature of humankind: it provided a coherent set of terms in which the unity and the diversity of humankind could be simultaneously analysed and coherently contemplated; it provided an intellectual and moral foundation for securely grounding important ideas concerning the unity of humankind, the moral equality of all human beings, and, within its dazzlingly diverse forms, the commonality or universality of the human condition. But even this was not enough. What modern anthropology ended up offering also proved an incomplete, partial and even compromised notion of human universalism.

Modern anthropology's failure was not in its own intellectual constructs. These were adequate to articulating a clear vision of the unity of humankind transcending the varieties of living human beings and the varying forms which the human condition has historically taken. But it is too much to expect any scholarly discipline, especially one more often remote from than allied to those who set the agendas of organized power, to refashion the world unaided in accordance with its own vision. Moreover, modern anthropology for too long failed to come to terms with its own social placement. Its intellectual message and moral potential became compromised, first, by its probably inescapable association, as a creature of Western civilization, with the West's dominating world-historical career (hence all the talk an academic generation ago about anthropology as 'the child of Western imperialism')[9]; and, second, by its problematic placement in a beleaguered quarter of the modern academy, where its basic posture has necessarily been defensive rather than world fashioning. Accordingly, it has largely failed to come to terms with its own historical nature and career and has responded instead to the challenges of history and advancing globalization by retreating into archaic notions of its own distinctiveness, peculiar intellectual mission and special research mystique ('fieldwork').

Whatever the reasons, modern anthropology too has suffered the same fate as its predecessors noted above. It has failed to create from its intellectual grasp and moral intuition of the generic human situation an effective form of human universalism; it has not succeeded in institutionalizing its insights in the form of practices and structures that embody the moral and analytical power of its inclusive intellectual vision. More than its predecessors, it has succeeded in articulating coherently its insights into and intimations of the unity of the human condition; but it has not saved its articulation of the ideal of human inclusiveness and universality from being distorted and corrupted by the impact of its own partial, sectional and compromised placement in its moral world of the late twentieth-century academy and the governance of contemporary scholarship – another false, or at least failed, universalism.

While the cases discussed above are notable, they provide no exhaustive itemization; on the contrary, the history of the human social imagination is replete with such false or failed universalisms. Every age, arguably, contributes its own links to this chain or lineage. The entire Enlightenment project, the postmodernists strenuously but all too simplistically contend, is nothing but a monstrous example of this political and moral deformation. Yet a clear example is provided by one of the Enlightenment's subsequent expressions or incarnations. The contrast between the sublime socialist vision of inclusive human solidarity, on the one hand, and the tawdry practices and institutional structures of 'actually existing socialism' in many of its historical forms, on the other, offers poignant testimony of the role played by compromised universalisms throughout the twentieth century. Each era seems to produce its own characteristic instances of this failure. The new global century just beginning may be no different.

Globalization: the next compromised universalism?

Much of the current globalization literature speaks of the creation through increasing economic interdependence of a single unified world. All this is made to sound as positive and as benign as it is said to be irresistible. But it does raise the question of what kind of world is being created, according to whose agenda and in whose interests, and how and in what form the new social order which an unchallengeable economic logic is said to be creating for us all is to be institutionalized. Behind these concerns, the image of a humankind at last unified by an emerging network of comprehensive and inclusive interdependence beckons; but is this image again one not of a genuine but of a spurious, deceptive and distorted universalism? The transformation which we are witnessing under the label of globalization may well be just the next in a line of false universalisms to which humankind has been asked to submit.

A good deal of scepticism is warranted on this point. After all, the whole globalization agenda in which we are asked to enlist rests simply on that earlier form of false universalism, that of the market. The difference is that now we are asked to submit totally to the operations and supremacy of market principles at the level of the entire world itself rather than, as before, of the sovereign state. As with the earlier false universalism of market impartiality, here again we need to ask in whose interests is this new world being created, whose sectional agenda stands to be advanced behind globalization's façade, its deceptive masquerade of impersonality as neutrality?

Yet against this negative assessment of what globalization may mean for the creation of one single integrated human community, we should not be insensitive to the possibility of a positive potential of truly historic significance for humankind within the now breakneck rush of the globalization process. George Soros has somewhere remarked that there already exists a global economy, but not yet a global society. If, in response to the former, the latter is now taking shape around us, or is about to, we need to be concerned about what kind of global society and human community is coming into being and on what principles it is based.

Whether it takes the form we may prefer or not, globalization processes are arguably now creating, for the first time in human history, the detailed social infrastructure of a single unified humanity, a universal human community: a network of mutual human interdependence and of worldwide involvement in one another's fate. It may, at worst, be the interdependence born merely of market principles, of those who have long dreamed of a world held together by nothing more noble than the dismal logic of comparative advantage in production; but even in this worst case, what is emerging nonetheless is a comprehensive form of human interdependence, unprecedented in its scope and grip. What will result will, of course, be the worst case unless in a concerted way – in the midst of the gamut of globalization processes and on the basis of understanding them deeply – people can together imagine, insist upon and somehow 'negotiate' something better.

While humankind may be at last effectively unified under these circumstances by the false universalism of mere market principles, what is occurring may still be of enormous historical significance for humankind. The profound issue involved here – behind the political, economic and communicative transformations which the modernist and postmodernist theories of globalization processes have identified – is a moral or philosophical one. It involves the question whether globalization processes are now producing, of whatever kind, a single interdependent human community and therefore, in whatever form, providing some objectively real foundation for the notion of the commonality and universality of the human condition.

No matter how hierarchical and inequitable the form of human inclusiveness and interdependence now being fashioned by globalization processes may be, they are still producing a world in which, for the first time, the unity of humankind of which religions and anthropologists have in their different ways imagined, dreamed, or intuited will have some objective basis. Such a development creates the possibility for something dramatic, novel and significant in the moral progress of humankind to occur; it represents a transformative moment in the history of the human moral imagination. For the first time, a sense of the unity and moral equality of humankind will no longer be a difficult matter of abstract moral intuition. Instead, as a result of advancing globalization processes, it will have a socially objective and material, an experiential and existential, foundation.

Noting that in the next twenty-five years there will be 2 billion more people coming onto the planet, virtually all of them living in the so-called developing countries, and recognizing that we and they will all be linked in a very direct and immediate way – by the air we breathe, by trade, by finance, by drugs, by health, by immigration, by peace, by war – World Bank President James Wolfensohn aptly captures the cumulative moral implications of this unfolding transformation of the worldwide human situation: 'In every way we are dealing in one planet', he observes (Hartcher 2000: 30–31). 'We're at a stage now where all of us have to understand that we are living as part of a global community. And this isn't some sort of strange philosophy. This is reality.'

This is a development whose significance should not be minimized. Where an awareness of the commonality of the human situation and the involvement of all of humankind in one another's lives is transformed from a moral intuition to an experiential reality grounded in a worldwide social infrastructure of interconnection, then something hugely important has happened. The unity of humankind may cease to be simply a slogan or idealistic aspiration and becomes, at least in principle and prospect, a lived social reality.

That is why ultimately, beyond the political-economic and communicative dimensions with which much of the relevant theories and literature are preoccupied, globalization is profoundly a moral, a philosophical, issue.

Of course, the emergence of a comprehensive and genuine sense of human interdependence and mutual moral involvement from these often unedifying processes of corporate-led economic globalization is far from guaranteed. As ever, things are open ended and contestable: that is, if not there simply for the taking, then there for people to make what best of it they can.[10] Whether the powerful interests promoting the form of globalization and advancing human interdependence which we are now experiencing will succeed in suppressing that new moral sense, or whether that new social and moral awareness of a universal human interdependence and common fate will emerge from the universalization of the grim logic of the 'dismal science', remains unclear. It is an open question whether that new historical and moral awareness will be contained, captured and thwarted by the new conflicts and hierarchies which corporate-led globalization often entails; or whether human beings will succeed in capturing from those developments, and from the morally equivocal world into which globalization processes are delivering us, not just the redeeming vision of the unity of humankind but some stake in and some hold upon a part of its emerging social infrastructure.

Michael Ignatieff discerningly articulates an important part of what this contemporary transformation of the human moral imagination entails when he notes (1999: 4–5, 8):

> It isn't obvious why strangers in peril halfway across the world *should* be our business. For most of human history, the boundaries of our moral universe were the borders of the tribe, language, religion, or nation. The idea that we might have obligations to human beings beyond our borders simply because we belong to the same species is a recent invention, the result of our awakening to the shame of having done so little to help the millions of strangers who died in this century's experiments in terror and extermination. Nothing good has come of these experiments except perhaps for the consciousness that we are all Shakespeare's 'thing itself': unaccommodated man, the poor, bare forked animal. It is 'the thing itself' that has become the subject – and the rationale – for the modern universal human rights culture ... Weak as the narrative of compassion and moral commitment may be, it is infinitely stronger than it was fifty

years ago. We are scarcely aware of the extent to which our moral imagination has been transformed since 1945 by the growth of a language and practice of moral universalism.[11]

This is no naïve idealism – a Polyanna vision of universal harmony delivered *deus ex machina* by an unexplained outbreak of ever-expanding goodwill – but the yield of sober, even grim, historical reflection upon the full horror and inhumanity of the century just ended. As Ignatieff further explains (ibid., 18–20):

> In the twentieth century, the idea of human universality rests less on hope than on fear, less on optimism about the human capacity for good than on dread of human capacity for evil, less on a vision of man as maker of his history than of man as wolf toward his own kind ... Modern universalism is built upon the experience of a new kind of crime: the crime against humanity ... Famine and ethnic war pulverize huge numbers of different individuals into exactly equal units of pure humanity [,] ... placed on the anvil of suffering and hammered into sameness and then into oblivion ... In this sense, human brotherhood is a myth made actual and concrete by the history of twentieth-century horror: it is a myth with a history, a necessity only history can give ... An ethic of universal moral obligation among strangers [becomes] a necessity for the future of life on the planet.

No weak 'herbivore' daydream in a world of savage 'carnivores', this reaching towards the recognition and actualization of human universality represents the emerging objective impulsion to contemplate, as Adorno counsels, a vast scene of despair from the standpoint of the possibility, even necessity, of redemption. Here in Ignatieff's compassionate yet altogether unsentimental meditation on our common history of modern inhumanity, we can see that new moral insight into the universality of the human condition, grounded in an intensifying mutual interrelatedness, being captured and redeemed from the worst that the modern history of global and globalized humankind can deliver us.

Notes

1 But, as James Mittelman has pointed out to me, this too may be an instance of an illusory cosmopolitanism or 'compromised universalism'. Overwhelmingly, this massive corpus of globalization literature has been produced by scholars in the dominant Euro-American world; substan-

tially if unacknowledgedly, it reflects the quite partial viewpoint and sectional interests of those countries and their academic classes, who are in many ways among the beneficiaries, the 'winners' rather than the 'losers', of globalization. All standpoints are to some degree partial and limited, all places are parochial. But, as any stranger who has ever lived in New York or London or Paris realizes, there is no parochialism like the parochialism of places that imagine themselves central.

2 The idea of time/space compression has been central to all of Giddens's writings about globalization and late modernity since the mid-1980s (such as Giddens 1990 and 1991) and features again in his 1999 BBC Reith Lectures entitled 'A Runaway World'. The same idea is also basic to Zygmunt Baumann's recent essay (1998).

3 In the case of the Muslim Malay villagers of the Malaysian state of Kelantan (as, I would argue, for most Muslims worldwide), the pilgrimage and fasting month rituals give expression to this elusive idea of the moral equality before God of all human beings and, at the same time, to the tension between this egalitarian vision of human common-ality and the implacable actualities of social inequality and division in mundane life (see Kessler 1978: 216–222 and 244–246, especially 218–220). No less poignant, analogous moments of ritual recognition of the equality of all believers before God and, at the same time, of how this idea is commonly belied in everyday experience – of the tensions between the idea of the moral equality of all human beings and the facts of social inequality – are also identifiable in both Judaism and Christianity. It is in ritual that ideal visions and unideal reality are brought together; ritual gives expression to both these dimensions of the human situation and to the irreconcilable tensions between them. That the idea of human equality and the notion of the abstract individual (in this case under God's law, as a yardstick against which all humans should measure them-selves morally) were born in the human imagination in a religious form, and were first launched into the world and human history under the sponsorship of religion, is a little recognized consequence, and part of the legacy, of monotheistic doctrine and faith.

4 Throughout Judaism, from its origins, Theodore Long (1991: 20–21) remarks, 'we find universalism entangled with particularism'. In its main themes, Hebrew religion 'contains seeds of universalism, but they are planted in a very particularistic soil which limited their full growth and flowering. In that sense at least, Israel's history is the story of univer-salism's struggle to grow in somewhat unfavourable conditions'. This view of ancient Judaism, especially in its prophetic variants, as the source of an emergent but not uncontested moral universalism was, of course, that of Max Weber (see Zeitlin 1984).

5 This, with all its attendant understandings and implicit theory, is the term for civilizational encounters or engagements which, notoriously and quite unhelpfully, the work of Samuel Huntington (1996) has made fash-ionable.

6 The kind of 'market fundamentalism' which is widely known in the United States as 'neoliberalism' is often referred to elsewhere (including in Australia) as 'economic rationalism'. See in particular Pusey (1991). On the 'genealogy' of the term 'economic rationalism', see Schneider

(1998). Less seriously, ever sardonically if at times tediously, see also Ellis (1998).

7 This is part of the peculiar power of such movements as Pauline Hanson's One Nation Party in Australia. The success of governments and parties championing the wholesale privatization of public assets and state facilities has rested, to a significant degree, on their ability to tap and mobilize electorally, on this very basis, the discontent of the principal victims of the 'deregulation' required by 'economic globalization', especially certain vulnerable and increasingly marginalized remnants of the old urban working class as well as those in various regional centres and non-metropolitan districts (centres of now declining industries that, as a result of the removal of old tariff protection, have become areas of catastrophic unemployment). Such people have arguably contributed most (especially in unemployment and declining social amenities and government facilities) to the economic restructuring of recent years and have generally received least from it. In this connection see Manne (1998, especially parts 2 and 3: 43–84 and 85–103).

8 For some further development of this point and its practical implications for questions of 'cultural identity' and the 'negotiation of difference' see Kessler (1985: especially 136–137; 1991: especially 61–64).

9 The classic source for these adverse characterizations is Kathleen Gough's often reprinted article (Gough 1968).

10 Despite its tendencies towards 'technological determinism' in the face of the new communications and information technologies, a recent work by the prominent Australian Labor Party politician Lindsay Tanner (1999) contends that, while globalization may be unavoidable, it is negotiable – one hopes he is right – and that it is accordingly the task of responsible states to negotiate the engagement of national structures with global forces. While the formula 'unavoidable but negotiable' is appealing, just how this is to be done, and what policies may be devised to further that end, remain unclear. That, perhaps, is the major challenge now facing social democracy in the new era of accelerating globalization.

11 For Ignatieff's account of 'the needs of strangers' and of the moral claims which they make upon us – based on his reading of the situation *in extremis* of Shakespeare's *King Lear*, and of elemental 'unaccommodated' humankind, 'the thing itself', as a 'bare forked animal' – see Ignatieff (1984).

3 Globalization and private capital movements

Rajah Rasiah[1]

Introduction

As with globalization itself, the debate on international private capital flows has long diverged in content.[2] A range of perceptions – from whole-hearted support to outright rejection – has evolved. Many take positions somewhere along the plank that links the two extremes. Others oscillate between one extreme and another depending on political circumstances. To believers, the globalization process has unleashed the transnational productive forces following the flow of consumption capital to every nook and cranny of the world. To critics, global private capital flows have been driven by specific locales and directed to particular locales. Hence, while technological change has made the world increasingly integrated, it has also been disembedding at the same time (see Polanyi 1957).[3] On the one hand, information and interactions have increased, and on the other hand, relationships between individuals have become more impersonal. The pattern of international private capital flows, in other words, continues to reproduce unequal relations and accumulation. The power asymmetry between peoples, firms and nations is exacerbated by the widening gap that has emerged with unequal information access (Dicken 1998).

This chapter examines international private capital movements across the globe. Consistent with the conceptualization of Polanyi (1957), the central thesis pursued in this chapter is that concentrations of power generally determine the topography of international private capital movements. Of significance to the chapter are the questions of origin and destination of international private capital movements. Related questions include the stages, phases, skill categories and institutional support characteristics of sites located in the international division of labour. Given the pervasive nature of neoliberal tenets, the chapter draws some implications for such theories. The chapter largely confines analysis to the factors that explain international private capital movements and selected indicators of development.

International private capital flows

Two types of international private capital flows are examined here, namely foreign direct investment (FDI) and foreign portfolio equity, and near equity investment and convertible bonds. The first refers to direct investment into companies, either totally or as joint ventures located across borders. The second generally refers to country funds, depository receipts and direct purchase of shares by foreign investors. Included in the last are less volatile investments such as convertible bonds. Aid flows – which are extremely important – were excluded to obtain a richer discussion. The overall contention in this section is that private capital flows demonstrate greater influence from the richer and more powerful capitalist economies – including the more advanced developing economies – demonstrating the significance of power relations involving economic agents. Unlike the typical core–periphery argument advanced by *dependentistas*, the absolute conditions of some of the captives need not worsen even if the gap from the captors continues to widen.

Foreign direct investment

FDI forms a major source of private capital outflows and inflows across the globe. While portfolio and related capital movements are not only faster but also larger in volume, in net terms the volume is smaller than FDI. FDI appears less footloose and more long term, for it requires registration and investment in physical assets. Besides, it also carries with it technological and trade consequences.

The figures on FDI flows show that developed economies not only account for the lion's share of FDI outflows, but also FDI inflows. The twenty developed economies among the ninety-eight economies reported in Table 3.1 accounted for at least 60 per cent of capital inflows and 84 per cent of capital outflows in the period 1975–1995. Since 1994 there has been a rise of FDI inflows from developing economies, which is largely a consequence of greater outflows from fast-growing developing economies such as South Korea, Singapore and Taiwan. The continued concentration of FDI flows among the developed economies and a select group of fast-growing developing economies supports Hirst and Thompson's (1996: 2) contention.

Overall, FDI flows across the globe have varied with the state of the global economy. International private capital movements have risen far more during periods of boom compared to periods of recession (see Table 3.1). Developing economies have enjoyed rising FDI inflows even during periods of global recession, which could be a consequence of the key FDI recipient economies enjoying rapid growth, during times of global recession. Average annual FDI inflows into developing economies in the recessionary periods of 1991–1992 and 1986–1990 rose from US$26.5 billion to US$45.6 billion, when that to the developed economies fell from US$131.8 billion to US$117.2 billion (UNCTAD 1998b: 266). There has also been a gradual rise in FDI inflows to the transitional economies of Central and Eastern Europe following the collapse of communism from 1989, with their share in world FDI inflows rising from 0.01 per cent in 1975–1977 to 4.00 per cent in 1995–1996.

Table 3.1   FDI inflows and outflows, 1975–1996

	Developed		Developing		Other Europe and Central Asia	
	Inflow	*Outflow*	*Inflow*	*Outflow*	*Inflow*	*Outflow*
1975–1977[a]	69.19	98.20	30.81	1.44	0.01	0.04
1979–1981[b]	69.17	97.72	30.64	2.28	0.04	0.02
1986–1990[b]	82.95	93.38	16.68	6.68	0.31	0.01
1991–1992[a]	70.48	92.44	27.42	7.51	2.04	0.03
1994	59.61	83.51	37.87	16.21	2.43	0.28
1995–1996[b]	62.18	85.47	33.79	14.35	4.00	0.15

Source: UNCTAD (1998), compiled from Annex Table A.3.

Notes:
[a] recession periods
[b] boom periods

Developed economies account for more of the world's FDI outflows than the developing economies, though the grip has loosened gradually. Developing economies' share rose from 1.4 per cent in 1975–1977 to 16.2 per cent in 1994 before dropping slightly to 14.4 per cent in 1995–1996. Unlike FDI inflows, FDI outflows from the developed economies have continued to rise. The situation has been similar in the developing economies (see UNCTAD 1998: 266).

Also, there is little relationship between FDI shares in gross fixed capital formation (GFCF) and the developmental status of developing economies. South Korea and Taiwan show very low levels of FDI in GFCF (see Table 3.2).[4] Singapore and Malaysia demonstrate high levels of FDI in GFCF. Oil-rich economies, such as Saudi Arabia and Venezuela, which enjoyed relatively high FDI levels in the 1960s and 1970s, have experienced a significant fall in relative contributions from the mid-1980s. Some economies such as war-torn Angola and Nigeria show high FDI/GFCF percentages not because of strong FDI inflows, but because of low overall GFCF.

FDI in developing economies is concentrated in resource-rich economies that are fairly politically stable, endowed with good infrastructure and demonstrate governance structures that are relatively capital-friendly. Low-wage unskilled labour is important, but is available as a ubiquitous resource in a number of developing economies. Its significance when seen alongside the other variables viewed above was relatively strong only until the late 1980s. The decomposition of production into value-added skills stages through Taylorist (see Froebel *et al.* 1980) and Fordist forms until at least the 1980s led to the transnationalization of production with unequal consequences as the dehumanizing stages generated considerable social tensions that were often met with authoritarian solutions. The transition to flexible forms in knowledge-based industries such as electronics has reversed such tendencies in Singapore and Malaysia.[5] Peripheral and semi-peripheral sites enjoyed little say in the decision making of transnationals under the Taylorist and Fordist milieu. Where flexible production forms have given rise to greater dispersal of organizational power as well as process innovation, local accumulation at peripheral sites has stimulated economic progress, albeit only in locations generating the requisite skills. Singapore, Taiwan, Penang (in Malaysia) and Hong Kong are a few of these sites where transnational capital expansion has demonstrated some features of systems-oriented clusterization tendencies (see Best 1999). The capacity of local regions – with strong state support – to engender improvements in institutional support has been important in the

Table 3.2   FDI in gross fixed capital formation, 1985–1995 (%)

	1985–1990	1990–1995		1985–1990	1990–1995
Algeria	0.1	0.1	Kenya	1.3	0.8
Angola	44.8	60.6	Korea R.	1.9	0.8
Argentina	13.0	17.6	Lebanon	3.7	0.6
Australia	11.2	9.3	Lesotho	6.0	2.4
Austria	3.0	1.8	Madagascar	4.5	4.3
Bangladesh	0.3	0.3	Malawi	6.2	4.6
Belgium	37.0	23.9	Malaysia	43.7	21.3
Benin	1.4	1.2	Mali	1.4	1.7
Bolivia	25.0	19.6	Mauritania	3.7	2.8
Brazil	3.1	2.7	Mauritius	4.5	1.9
Bulgaria	0.4	3.2	Mexico	16.9	10.5
Burkina Faso	0.5	0.8	Morocco	8.5	6.5
Burundi	0.6	0.7	Mozambique	3.8	3.1
Cameroon	0.0	2.2	Namibia	22.9	14.0
Canada	6.6	6.0	Nepal	0.7	0.6
CAR	-2.1	-2.3	Netherlands	20.2	12.6
Chad	3.0	8.2	New Zealand	27.7	25.5
Chile	21.5	9.2	Nicaragua	6.8	7.6
China	14.5	16.3	Niger	3.8	1.8
Hong Kong	12.2	6.7	Nigeria	34.9	36.6
Columbia	17.0	11.0	Norway	4.5	3.7
Congo DR	6.4	9.2	Oman	5.9	5.0
Congo R	na	1.1	Pakistan	5.1	4.3
Costa Rica	26.5	17.6	Panama	24.4	10.8
Côte d'Ivoire	-0.6	-2.3	Paraguay	11.3	8.3
Denmark	13.3	11.7	Peru	15.5	14.7
Dominican R	11.4	7.5	Philippines	13.6	7.4
Ecuador	14.6	12.3	PNG	27.9	18.5
Egypt	3.1	7.3	Poland	9.6	10.0
El Salvador	2.9	1.9	Portugal	17.7	8.0
Ethiopia	0.3	0.4	Romania	1.1	3.9
Finland	3.0	4.8	Russia	0.1	0.9
France	10.3	7.7	Rwanda	1.0	1.0
Gabon	0.4	-1.0	Saudi Arabia	1.7	-0.1
Ghana	17.8	11.8	Senegal	5.8	4.2
Greece	9.0	5.2	Sierra Leone	5.7	-3.3
Guatemala	8.4	5.7	Singapore	59.3	23.3
Guinea-Bissau	2.2	2.8	South Africa	0.7	0.5
Haiti	2.1	2.0	Trinidad and Tobago	31.2	44.6
Honduras	6.4	5.3	Tunisia	14.7	9.3
Hungary	33.3	29.5	Turkey	3.5	2.0
India	1.2	1.5	UAE	1.2	1.3
Indonesia	7.6	4.3	Uganda	8.4	8.9
Ireland	23.1	16.8	UK	13.7	10.0
Israel	8.4	4.0	Uruguay	11.1	4.9
Italy	2.6	1.5	USA	5.3	4.2
Jamaica	16.3	11.1	Venezuela	8.3	8.5
Japan	0.2	0.2	Zambia	27.2	13.0
Jordan	1.2	0.3	Zimbabwe	1.8	1.8

Source: Compiled from UNCTAD (1998).

formation of dynamic clusters. However, the gap in systems integration sophistication with leading US firms such as Intel is still wide. The bulk of the developing economies are not even approaching such potential.

Flexibilization has also taken on casual forms, dehumanizing workers or reducing workers' skills levels vertically, with the resultant vacuum replaced by energy-sapping multitasking, making workers temporary and easily replaceable (Deyo 1989). Most developing sites gripped with poor labour organization and legal instruments as well as weak governance continue to be subjected to such low levels of industrial restructuring. Under such circumstances, transnational corporations, with decision making centred at headquarters and parent sites, still condition the operations of subsidiaries in developing economies.

International organizations that address private capital flows encourage the provision of conditions attractive to capital, even under circumstances harmful to the interests of labour. Many of these organizations assume that capital inflows at extreme costs, however dislocating, are an important precondition for the progressive uplifting of the living standards of the masses at host sites. Hence, the World Bank and IMF urged developing economies to restructure their legal instruments, including labour and industrial relations policies that can attract FDI, which, *inter alia*, saw the mushrooming of export processing zones. The reach of the World Bank and IMF has been so pervasive that International Labour Organization (ILO) conventions, even when ratified by host governments, have been violated in order to stimulate FDI. China has often been criticized for using prison labour; India, Pakistan and Bangladesh for allowing child labour; and Indonesia, Malaysia, and Thailand for blocking labour organization (see Rasiah and Chua 1998). Yet, capital flows have been 'managed internationally' to access dehumanized labour in underdeveloped locations to meet the interests of capital competing for even small profits.

While many intervening host governments have a disastrous record of authoritarianism, developing economies (with the exception of Hong Kong) with high FDI participation and strong long-term growth, such as Singapore and Malaysia, have also demonstrated a pro-active role by the government. The data point to the centrality of the relevance of the nation-state in engendering and sustaining domestic growth, and to the spillover of international private capital's operations to the host country.

The formation of the World Trade Organization (WTO) in 1995 and subsequent efforts to tie international investment issues directly to trade have added new dimensions to global capital movements. The institution of Trade-Related Investment Measures (TRIM), which forbids trade-balancing investment measures, obviously calls for the removal of government intervention that is viewed as discriminatory to ownership attributes. Previous attempts to bulldoze through the Multilateral Agreement on Investment (MAI), now blocked though they could resurface, are increasingly viewed as aggravating further the power asymmetry between international capital and weaker nation-states. Domestic interests, thus, can be affected. However, many of the critics have questioned authoritarian governments' attempts to shield inefficient domestic firms. Dissipation of sugar rents in the Philippines until the mid-1980s, automobile rents in India and steel rents in Malaysia and Indonesia are examples. FDI movements abroad have been driven by the relative advantages of off-shore sites over parent sites. The major attractions include domestic markets (e.g. Volkswagen in China and Toyota in Thailand and Indonesia), tax holidays and other benefits, such as a malleable and literate workforce in environments endowed with good infrastructure, political stability and bureaucratic efficiency (e.g. Motorola, Intel and Advanced Micro Devices in Malaysia). A complex myriad of factors influenced relocation abroad, rather than any single factor (Rasiah 1990; Henderson 1990). In many cases, push factors, such as improved environmental standards (e.g. Asian Rare Earth from Japan to Malaysia in the 1980s) and labour standards (Siemens from Germany to Malaysia in the 1970s) in developed economies, were also more important in FDI movements abroad.

The choice of technology used by transnational corporations has also increasingly departed from factor endowments of host locations. Advances in information technology and the transformation of production from old-fashioned Taylorist forms to flexible, cellular and modularized systems using programmed intelligence have enhanced the role of knowledge workers in several industries. Also, their importance has permeated the electronics industry to propel most other industries. Hence, through entrepreneurial techno-deepening and diversification within firms, effective interfirm and institutional support from regional networks that are fairly open, host-site factor mixes are increasingly being reshaped to meet the needs of transnational operations abroad. However, host sites not responding to such demands required by competition and the demands of transnational corporations have increasingly figured less in their operations.

Singapore, Hong Kong and, to a lesser extent, Malaysia managed to upgrade and hence remain as important transnational sites. Intel moved out of Barbados and Schlumberger from Indonesia in the mid-1980s because of their failure to meet the changing requirements of international capital. In several chip manufacturing processes, miniaturization has evolved so much that human hands can no longer substitute for robotics. Hence, the prospects of most developing economies, which are entrenched in underdeveloped and stagnant regional dynamics, for attracting FDI have become increasingly remote.

By relying heavily on natural resources, some developing economies have managed to raise per capita income strongly in the past. International private capital has been drawn to such resource-rich sites for the extraction of minerals (e.g. copper in Chile and Zambia) or cash crop agriculture (e.g. bananas in the Caribbean and Philippines). Oil-rich economies such as Saudi Arabia, Kuwait and Venezuela experienced high per capita growth rates in the 1970s due to sharply rising oil prices, particularly following the oil crises of 1973–1975 and 1979–1980, when oil prices rose by 4.0 and 2.5 times respectively. Given the fall in oil prices and the virtual stagnation of other primary and secondary sectors, most oil-rich economies show slow growth in per capita income from the mid-1980s.

Foreign portfolio equity investment

While FDI flows have often dominated investment in developing economies, a number of emerging markets have experienced a sudden surge of portfolio equity and related inflows. The World Bank defines portfolio equity investment to include country funds, depository receipts and direct purchases of shares by foreign investors. Indeed, the individualization of transactions and relationships occurring alongside increased information and communication flows has enabled individuals to invest with increasing pace across the globe. At one level, the liberalization process has been disembedding, but at another level the increased reach of individuals from better communication networks has reduced space.

Portfolio equity capital flows are influenced considerably by confidence and the state of development of capital markets in recipient economies. Hence, East and Southeast Asian economies experienced a sharp rise in foreign investment in stock markets only after they were promoted aggressively from the mid-1980s. However, the promotions were not accompanied by improvements in governance mechanisms. Political stability and rapid growth had helped inflate bullish sentiments until the financial crisis struck. Prior to that, foreign equity in stock markets was negligible in Indonesia, Malaysia, the Philippines, Taiwan and South Korea.

As can be seen in Table 3.3, the share of foreign portfolio investment, near equity securities and convertible bonds in total foreign investment to developing economies soared in the period 1986–1995. As a proportion of net FDI, portfolio equity and related flows to the emerging markets rose from 4.7 per cent in 1986 to 41.5 per cent in 1993 before falling to 26.9 per cent in 1995. The commensurate figures for Asia rose from 4.8 per cent in 1986 to 33.0 per cent in 1993 before falling to 24.1 per cent in 1995. The share of portfolio and related capital flows to Latin America in relation to net FDI rose sharply from none in 1986 to 58.8 per cent in 1993 before falling to 21.9 per cent in 1995. The share of portfolio equity and related investment in FDI to Africa and the Middle East increased from none in 1991 to 43.3 per cent in 1995. The transition economies of Europe and Central Asia have also experienced an increase from none in 1987 to 81.2 per cent in 1994.

Non-FDI inflows have increasingly become notoriously harmful to small open economies. Restrictions on hot money movements were recommended by Keynes, the chief architect of the Bretton Woods institutions, the World Bank and IMF. Particularly small open economies have become extremely vulnerable to speculative attacks as can be seen from the Asian meltdown. The 1997 ravages by speculative capital on the Thai baht and its subsequent contagion of other regional currencies are the latest damaging forays by volatile non-FDI capital movements. Annual exports and forex transactions in 1977 reached US$1.3 trillion and US$4.6 trillion,

Table 3.3 Portfolio equity capital and related flows to emerging markets as proportion of net FDI, 1986–1995

	1986	1987	1988	1989	1990	1991	1992	1993	1994	1995
Emerging markets	4.7	3.0	4.4	10.4	9.4	20.1	19.4	41.5	34.7	26.9
Asia	4.8	3.8	5.2	15.2	9.5	13.7	11.7	33.0	31.9	24.1
Africa and Middle East	0.0	0.0	0.0	0.0	0.0	0.0	0.0	2.0	16.5	43.3
Latin America	0.0	0.9	1.8	4.9	11.0	29.5	31.7	58.7	40.2	21.9
Europe and Central Asia		0.0	76.0	53.4	67.5	62.6	24.3	67.7	81.2	76.8

Source: UNCTAD (1998)

respectively. World exports and forex transactions rose to US$4.8 trillion and US$325 trillion respectively, in 1995 (Korten, cited in Khor 1997: 15). Indeed, the amount of currency turnover unassociated with exports had risen from 78.7 per cent in 1977 to 98.5 per cent in 1995.

Since portfolio equity capital in markets with no controls enjoys fluidity to move quickly, its quicksilver flights sometimes disrupt the financial health of corporations. Legal instruments in developed economies often prevent a run on shareholders' equity. With poorly conceived and inadequately developed institutional instruments, developing economies have often faced volatile attacks from portfolio equity capital movements across the globe. In several developing economies, capital markets have evolved too quickly without concomitant developments in the instruments of corporate governance. The vulnerability of individual economies to unfettered speculative attacks becomes higher when their size is small. The United States not only enjoys capital market development beyond the capability of a few speculators to undermine in the short run, but its economic size also ensures that the dollar is seldom subjected to speculative attacks. The fear of losing values from currency runs has often attracted bearish responses from capital market investors in developing economies. The 1997 Asian financial crisis is a classic example of the effects of speculative storms on ineffectively governed small open economies. Given the security offered by large developed economies, giant speculators often seek a cushion in such sites. Even in a number of developing economies where non-governmental organizations have sought the tightening of capital market operations to prevent runs and other forms of abuse, the political elite – long fed through patronage – has proven its resolve by stubbornly opposing reforms. Hence, capital market internationalization under prevailing circumstances has only exacerbated the stark differences between the developed and developing economies.

Stock and currency markets have become more vulnerable following increased liberalization across developing economies. Three of the four Asian newly industrialized economies (NIEs), i.e. Singapore, South Korea and Taiwan, were forced to intensify their liberalization efforts since the Plaza Accord of 1985, while the formation of the WTO and related regional groupings has quickened the application of these policies. Fully convertible exchange rates have opened up developing economies to volatile fluctuations. The uncertainty associated with uncontrolled currency markets also exposes sharp fluctuations in asset/liability ratios when the former is denominated in local currencies and the latter in strong foreign currencies. Apart from massive capital flight and fallen domestic demand, South Korea, Indonesia, Malaysia and Thailand faced a liquidity crisis in 1997 as a consequence of sharply bloated liabilities denominated in foreign currencies. Taiwan and Singapore managed to minimize the regional contagion following interventions by their governments to shield their currency and stock markets.

Foreign capital flows have been dictated by the interest of capital rather than host sites. Spatial capital movements – from both developed and developing economies – have been determined by the attractiveness of host sites for resource and market appropriation. Stock markets have unravelled the systemic frailties of dominance by capital emerging from the captors, exposing weak economies to substantial damage.

Implications for development

Central to this chapter is Polanyi's (1957) contention that power relations determine economic relations. The economic implications to expect are that the consequences of private capital flows will continue to widen the gap between the captors and the larger mass of captives. Thus, while the absolute conditions of a number of developing economies could improve following private capital inflows, the relative position of most of them will continue to worsen. Also, where developing economies demonstrate improvements in their relative gap with the developed economies, the exceptions generally arise from the domestic policies of the captives aimed at engendering progress rather than from the interests of the captors. The role of international private capital flows in development has often raised strong passions. While it is clear that foreign capital is attracted mainly to the more developed economies (Hirst and Thompson 1996), the factors explaining their size and direction are not clear. Despite the lack of a relationship between FDI flows and per capita income levels, high- and middle-income economies attract the most FDI inflows. Other factors, such as political stability, proximity to big markets, financial incentives, human capital endowments and infra-structure are also important.

Given the emphasis in Ishak Shari's chapter on poverty and inequality, this chapter will confine its assessment to GDP growth rates and per capita income differentials, as well as selected quality of life indicators. The first allows for per capita income inequality between economies without discussing income inequality trends between individuals. While preventing assessments involving the widening tendencies of income differentials under capitalism, the analysis does allow an examination of per capita income inequality trends between national economies.

GDP growth seems little correlated with levels of FDI participation in GFCF across the globe. In the consecutive periods of 1980–1990 and 1990–1997, China, India, Indonesia, Malaysia, Mauritius, Oman, Singapore, South Korea, Taiwan and Thailand recorded average annual GDP growth rates exceeding 5 per cent (see Table 3.4). China's achievement was the most spectacular: in both periods its average annual GDP growth rate exceeded 10 per cent. China, Oman, Malaysia and Singapore show strong FDI participation in GFCF. Except for Oman, which relies strongly on extractive industries, export-oriented manufacturing has been important in the others. Government intervention has been strong in all these export-oriented manufacturing economies. However, India and South Korea show extremely low levels of FDI participation. The same can be said of Taiwan. Government intervention has also been strong in these economies.

Egypt enjoyed an average annual GDP growth rate exceeding 5 per cent in 1980–1990. Chile, El Salvador, Lesotho, Mozambique, Nicaragua, Papua New Guinea, Syria and Uganda recorded average annual GDP growth rate exceeding 5 per cent in 1990–1997. Only Chile and Uganda showed FDI participation in GFCF exceeding 8 per cent. Papua New Guinea, Namibia, Trinidad and Tobago, the Philippines, Mexico, Tunisia, Uruguay and Zambia show high FDI participation rates in GFCF, but achieved low or negative GDP growth in at least one of the two periods. Even a scatter diagram does not show a clear pattern of relationship, suggesting the possibility of a strong influence from more dynamic intervening variables.[6]

The growing distance between the developed economies and the developing economies in per capita terms is shown in Table 3.4. Of the eighty-three developing economies reported in the table, only eleven showed per capita improvements relative to that of the developed economies' mean over the period 1980–1997. Two of these economies were located in South America, one in Central America and one in Africa. The two from South America, i.e. Argentina and Peru, show strong levels of FDI participation in GFCF (see Tables 3.2 and 3.4). The one from Central America, i.e. El Salvador, shows low levels of FDI participation in GFCF. The one from Africa, i.e. Gabon, had extremely low levels of FDI participation in GFCF.

The other eight, i.e. China, Hong Kong, Indonesia, Israel, Malaysia, Singapore, South Korea, Sri Lanka and Thailand, are

Table 3.4 GDP growth rates (%), PCIs (US$) and PCI differentials (%), 1980–1997

	Annual average growth (GDP)		GNP per capita			PCI/PCI$_{Switz}$			PCI/PCI$_{DEM}$		
	1980–1990	1990–1997	1980	1989	1997	1980	1989	1997	1980	1989	1997
Algeria	2.8	0.8	1870	2230	1490	11.4	7.5	3.4	18.1	12.2	5.8
Angola	3.7	0.7	470	610	340	2.9	2.0	0.87	4.6	3.3	1.3
Argentina	-0.3	4.5	2390	2160	8570	14.5	7.2	19.3	23.2	11.8	33.4
Australia	3.4	3.7	9820	14,360	20,540	59.7	48.1	46.3	95.2	78.3	79.9
Austria	2.2	1.6	10,230	17,300	27,980	62.2	57.9	63.1	99.1	94.4	108.9
Bangladesh	4.3	4.5	130	180	270	0.8	0.6	0.6	1.3	1.0	1.1
Belgium	1.9	1.2	12,180	16,220	26,420	74.1	54.3	59.6	118.0	88.5	102.8
Benin	3.2	4.5	310	380	380	1.9	1.3	0.9	3.0	2.1	1.5
Bolivia	-0.2	3.8	570	620	950	3.5	2.1	2.1	5.5	3.4	3.7
Brazil	2.8	3.1	2050	2540	4720	12.5	8.5	10.7	19.9	13.9	18.4
Bulgaria	4.0	-3.5	4150	2320	1140	25.2	7.8	2.6	40.2	12.7	4.4
Burkina Faso	3.7	3.3	210	320	240	1.3	1.1	0.5	2.0	1.8	0.9
Burundi	4.4	-3.5	200	220	180	1.2	0.7	0.4	1.9	1.2	0.7
Cameroon	3.3	0.1	670	1000	650	4.1	3.4	1.5	6.5	5.5	2.5
Canada	3.4	2.1	10,130	19,030	19,290	61.6	63.7	43.5	98.2	103.8	75.1
CAR	1.4	1.2	300	390	320	1.8	1.3	0.7	2.9	2.1	1.3
Chad	3.8	1.8	120	190	240	0.7	0.6	0.5	1.2	1.0	0.9
Chile	4.1	7.2	2150	1770	5020	13.1	5.9	11.3	20.8	9.7	19.5
China	10.2	11.9	290	350	860	1.8	1.2	1.9	2.8	1.9	3.4
Hong Kong	6.9	5.3	4240	10,350	25,280	25.8	34.6	57.0	41.1	56.5	98.4

Table 3.4 Continued:

	Annual average growth (GDP)		GNP per capita			PCI/PCI$_{Switz}$			PCI/PCI$_{DEM}$		
	1980–1990	1990–1997	1980	1989	1997	1980	1989	1997	1980	1989	1997
Colombia	3.7	4.5	1180	1200	2280	7.2	4.0	5.1	11.4	6.6	8.9
Congo DR	1.6	-6.6	220	260	110	1.3	0.9	0.3	2.1	1.4	0.4
Congo R	3.6	0.7	900	940	660	5.5	3.2	1.5	8.7	5.1	2.6
Costa Rica	3.0	3.7	1730	1780	2640	10.5	6.0	6.0	6.8	9.7	10.3
Côte d'Ivoire	0.9	3.0	1150	790	690	7.0	2.6	1.6	11.1	4.3	2.7
Denmark	2.4	2.3	12,950	20,450	32,500	78.8	68.4	73.3	125.5	111.6	126.5
Dominican R	3.0	5.0	1160	790	1670	7.1	2.6	3.7	11.2	4.3	6.5
Ecuador	2.0	3.1	1270	1020	1590	7.7	3.4	3.6	12.3	5.6	6.2
Egypt	5.3	3.9	580	640	1180	3.5	2.1	2.7	5.6	3.5	4.6
El Salvador	0.2	5.8	660	1070	1810	4.0	3.6	4.1	6.4	5.8	7.0
Ethiopia	2.3	4.5	140	120	110	0.9	0.4	0.3	1.4	0.7	0.4
Finland	3.3	1.1	9720	22,120	24,080	59.1	74.0	54.3	94.2	120.7	93.7
France	2.4	1.3	11,730	17,820	26,050	71.4	59.6	58.8	113.7	97.2	101.4
Gabon	0.6	2.6	na	2960	4230	na	9.9	9.5	na	16.2	16.5
Ghana	3.0	4.3	420	390	370	2.6	1.3	0.8	4.07	2.1	1.4
Greece	1.8	1.8	4380	5350	12,010	26.6	17.9	27.1	42.4	29.2	46.7
Guatemala	0.8	4.1	1080	910	1500	6.6	3.1	3.4	10.5	4.96	5.8
Guinea-Bissau	4.0	3.8	na	na	240	na	na	0.5	na	na	0.9
Haiti	-0.2	-3.8	270	360	330	1.6	1.2	0.7	2.6	2.0	1.3

Honduras	2.7	3.4	560	900	700	3.4	3.0	1.6	5.4	4.9	2.7
Hungary	1.6	-0.4	4180	2590	4430	25.4	8.7	10.0	40.5	14.1	17.2
India	5.8	5.9	240	340	390	1.5	1.1	0.9	2.3	1.9	1.5
Indonesia	6.1	7.5	430	500	1110	2.6	1.7	2.5	4.2	2.7	4.3
Ireland	3.2	6.5	4880	8710	18,280	29.7	29.2	41.3	47.3	47.5	71.1
Israel	3.5	6.4	4500	9790	15,810	27.4	32.8	35.7	43.6	53.4	61.5
Italy	2.4	1.1	6480	15,120	20,120	39.4	50.6	45.4	62.8	82.5	78.3
Jamaica	2.0	0.8	1040	1260	1560	6.3	4.2	3.5	10.1	6.9	6.1
Japan	4.0	1.4	9890	23,810	37,850	60.2	79.7	85.4	95.8	129.9	147.3
Jordan	2.6	7.2	1420	1640	1570	8.6	5.5	3.5	13.8	9.0	6.1
Kenya	4.2	2.0	420	360	330	2.6	1.2	0.7	4.1	2.0	1.3
Korea R	9.5	7.2	1520	4400	10,550	9.3	14.7	23.8	14.7	24.0	41.1
Lebanon	78.2	8.3	na	na	3350	na	na	7.6	na	na	13.0
Lesotho	4.3	7.6	420	470	670	2.6	1.6	1.5	4.1	2.6	2.6
Madagascar	1.1	0.8	350	230	250	2.1	0.8	0.6	3.4	1.3	1.0
Malawi	2.3	3.6	230	180	220	1.4	0.6	0.5	2.2	1.0	0.9
Malaysia	5.2	8.7	1620	2160	4680	9.9	7.2	10.6	15.7	11.8	18.2
Mali	2.9	3.3	190	270	260	1.2	0.9	0.6	1.8	1.5	1.0
Mauritania	1.7	4.3	440	500	450	2.7	1.7	1.0	4.3	2.7	1.8
Mauritius	6.2	5.1	na	1990	3800	na	6.7	8.6	na	10.9	14.8
Mexico	1.1	1.8	2090	2010	3680	12.7	6.7	8.3	20.3	11.0	14.3
Morocco	4.2	2.0	900	880	1250	5.5	3.0	2.8	8.7	4.8	4.9
Mozambique	1.7	6.9	230	80	90	1.4	0.3	0.2	2.2	0.4	0.4
Namibia	1.3	4.1	na	1030	2220	na	3.5	5.0	na	5.6	8.6
Nepal	4.6	5.0	140	180	210	0.9	0.6	0.5	1.4	1.0	0.8
Netherlands	2.3	2.3	11,470	15,920	25,820	69.8	53.3	58.3	111.1	86.9	100.5

Table 3.4 Continued:

	Annual average growth (GDP)		GNP per capita			PCI/PCI$_{Switz}$			PCI/PCI$_{DEM}$		
	1980–1990	1990–1997	1980	1989	1997	1980	1989	1997	1980	1989	1997
New Zealand	1.7	3.2	7090	12,070	16,480	43.2	40.4	37.2	68.7	65.9	64.1
Nicaragua	-2.6	5.7	740	na	410	4.5	na	0.9	7.2	na	1.6
Niger	0.1	1.5	330	290	200	2.0	1.0	0.5	3.2	1.6	0.8
Nigeria	1.6	2.7	1010	250	260	6.1	0.8	0.6	9.8	1.4	1.0
Norway	2.8	3.9	12,650	22,290	36,090	77.0	74.6	81.4	122.6	121.6	140.4
Oman	8.3	6.0	na	5220	4950	na	17.5	11.2	na	28.5	19.3
Pakistan	6.3	4.4	300	370	490	1.8	1.2	1.1	2.9	2.0	1.9
Panama	0.5	4.8	1730	1760	3080	10.5	5.9	7.0	16.7	9.6	12.0
Paraguay	2.5	3.1	1300	1030	2010	7.9	3.5	4.5	12.6	5.6	7.8
Peru	-0.3	6.0	930	1010	2460	5.7	3.4	5.6	9.0	5.5	9.6
Philippines	1.0	3.3	690	710	1220	4.2	2.4	2.8	6.7	3.9	4.8
PNG	1.9	7.6	780	890	940	4.7	3.0	2.1	7.6	4.9	3.7
Poland	1.8	3.9	3900	1790	3590	23.7	6.0	8.1	37.8	9.8	14.0
Portugal	2.9	1.7	2370	4250	10,450	14.4	14.2	23.6	23.0	23.2	40.7
Romania	0.5	na	2340	na	1420	14.2	na	3.2	22.7	na	5.5
Russia	2.8	-9	na	na	2740	na	na	6.2	na	na	10.7
Rwanda	2.5	-6.3	200	320	210	1.2	1.1	0.5	1.9	1.8	0.8
Saudi Arabia	-1.2	1.7	11,230	6020	6790	68.3	20.2	15.3	108.8	32.8	26.4

Senegal	3.1	2.4	450	650	550	2.7	2.2	1.2	4.4	3.6	2.1
Sierra Leone	0.6	-3.3	280	220	200	1.7	0.7	0.5	2.7	1.2	0.8
Singapore	6.6	8.5	4430	10,450	32,940	27.0	35.0	74.3	42.9	57.0	128.2
South Africa	1.2	1.5	2300	2470	3400	14.0	8.3	7.7	22.3	13.5	13.2
Spain	3.2	1.6	5400	9330	14,510	32.9	31.2	32.7	52.3	50.9	56.5
Sri Lanka	4.2	4.9	270	430	800	1.6	1.4	1.8	2.6	2.4	3.1
Sweden	2.3	0.9	13,520	21,570	26,220	82.2	72.2	59.2	131.0	117.7	102.0
Switzerland	2.2	-0.1	16,440	29,880	44,320	100.0	100.0	100.0	159.3	163.0	172.5
Syria	1.5	6.9	1340	980	1150	8.2	3.3	2.6	13.0	5.4	4.5
Thailand	7.6	7.5	670	1220	2800	4.1	4.1	6.3	6.5	6.7	10.9
Togo	1.6	2.2	410	390	330	2.5	1.3	0.7	4.0	2.1	1.3
Trinidad and Tobago	-2.5	1.5	4370	3230	4230	26.6	10.8	9.5	42.3	17.6	16.5
Tunisia	3.3	4.8	1310	1260	2090	8.0	4.2	4.7	12.7	6.9	8.1
Turkey	5.3	3.6	1470	1370	3130	8.9	4.6	7.1	14.2	7.5	12.2
UAE	-2.0	3.4	26,850	18,430	17,360	163.3	61.7	39.2	260.2	100.6	67.6
Uganda	3.1	7.2	300	250	320	1.8	0.8	0.7	2.9	1.4	1.3
UK	3.2	1.9	7920	14,610	20,710	48.1	48.9	46.7	76.7	79.7	80.6
Uruguay	0.4	3.7	2810	2620	6020	17.1	8.8	13.6	27.2	14.3	23.4
USA	2.9	2.5	11,360	20,910	28,740	69.1	70.0	64.9	110.1	114.1	111.8
Venezuela	1.1	1.9	3630	2450	3450	22.1	8.2	7.8	35.2	13.4	13.4
Zambia	0.8	-0.5	560	390	380	3.4	1.3	0.9	5.4	2.1	1.5
Zimbabwe	3.4	2.0	630	650	750	3.8	2.2	1.7	6.1	3.6	2.9

Source: Computed from World Bank, *World Development Report* (various issues).

Notes: PCI – Per Capita Income; PCI$_{DFM}$ – Developed Economies' Mean PCI; PCI$_{SWITZ}$ – Switzerland's PCI.

located in Asia. China, Malaysia and Singapore show high levels of FDI participation in GFCF. Hong Kong and Indonesia show relatively strong levels of FDI participation in GFCF in the period 1985–1990, but not very significantly in the period 1990–1995.

The divergence becomes even sharper when the per capita incomes of developing economies are taken as a percentage of Switzerland's, which has the world's highest per capita income (PCI). The gap between the rich and the poor has widened. The gradual decline of social democracies and rampant application of liberal policy instruments have even had an impact on South Korea, Taiwan, Japan and Malaysia, which had experienced improvements in social policy over a number of decades, but are now faced with worsening inequalities. The Gini coefficient measuring income inequality in South Korea and Taiwan began to worsen in the 1980s, in Malaysia since 1990 (see Rasiah 1996). The rising divergence suggests that capitalist development has generally been uneven and unequal.

Unlike typical neo-Marxist arguments (e.g. Baran 1973) which depict continuous underdevelopment of the periphery, the prime contention from the analysis in this section is that with the exception of a few nations, the material inequalities between the captors and captives should widen. Using two important proxies on material living conditions, i.e. infant mortality rates and access to primary school education, it can be argued that the general levels of living standards for most economies have improved. Of the 101 economies reported in Table 3.5, the infant mortality rates of only the Republic of Congo, Venezuela and Zambia rose in the period 1980–1996. Enrolment in primary school education of only Australia, Hong Kong, France, Hungary, Republic of Korea, Lesotho, Nicaragua, Poland and Trinidad and Tobago fell in the period 1980–1995 (see Table 3.5). Being generally developed, the rates for Australia, Republic of Korea, France, Hong Kong, Poland and Hungary were near universal. The upper middle-income economies of South Korea and Hong Kong had lower rates of participation in the 1950s.

While the general trend demonstrates significant material improvements, the extremely high levels of infant mortality faced by economies such as Sierra Leone, Guinea-Bissau, Lesotho, Madagascar, Malawi, Mali, Mozambique, Niger, Rwanda, Uganda and Zambia seriously disadvantage them from participating better in the development process. The young in these economies also enjoy little access to essential education. Yet these developments show little relationship with private international capital movements, neither FDI nor portfolio equity capital.

Table 3.5   Selected quality of life indicators, 1985–1996

	Infant mortality rate (per 1000 births)		Primary school enrolment (% of age group)	
	1980	*1996*	*1980*	*1995*
Algeria	98	32	81	95
Angola	153	124	70	na
Argentina	26	16	na	na
Australia	11	6	100	98
Austria	14	5	99	100
Bangladesh	132	77	na	na
Belgium	12	7	97	98
Benin	120	87	na	59
Bolivia	118	67	79	na
Brazil	67	36	80	90
Bulgaria	20	16	96	97
Burkina Faso	121	98	15	31
Burundi	121	97	20	52
Cameroon	94	54	na	na
Canada	10	6	na	95
CAR	117	96	56	na
Chad	147	115	na	na
Chile	32	12	na	86
China	42	33	na	99
Hong Kong	11	4	95	91
Colombia	45	25	na	85
Congo DR	111	90	na	61
Congo R	89	90	96	na
Costa Rica	20	12	89	92
Côte d'Ivoire	108	84	na	na
Denmark	8	6	96	99
Dominican R	74	40	na	81
Ecuador	67	34	na	92
Egypt	120	53	na	89
El Salvador	81	34	na	79
Ethiopia	155	109	na	24
Finland	8	4	na	99
France	10	5	100	99
Gabon	116	87	na	na
Germany	12	5	na	100
Ghana	100	71	na	na
Greece	18	8	103	na
Guatemala	81	41	58	na

Table 3.5 Continued

	Infant mortality rate (per 1000 births)		Primary school enrolment (% of age group)	
	1980	*1996*	*1980*	*1995*
Guinea-Bissau	168	134	47	na
Haiti	123	74	38	na
Honduras	70	44	78	90
Hungary	23	11	95	93
India	116	65	na	na
Indonesia	90	49	88	97
Ireland	11	5	100	100
Israel	15	6	na	na
Italy	15	6	na	97
Jamaica	21	12	96	100
Japan	8	4	100	100
Jordan	41	30	93	na
Kenya	72	57	91	na
Korea R	26	9	100	99
Lebanon	48	31	na	na
Lesotho	108	74	66	65
Madagascar	138	88	na	na
Malawi	169	133	43	100
Malaysia	30	11	na	91
Mali	184	120	20	25
Mauritania	120	94	na	60
Mauritius	32	17	79	96
Mexico	51	32	na	100
Morocco	99	53	62	72
Mozambique	155	123	36	40
Namibia	90	61	na	92
Nepal	132	85	na	na
Netherlands	9	5	93	99
New Zealand	13	6	100	100
Nicaragua	90	44	98	83
Niger	150	118	21	na
Nigeria	99	78	na	na
Norway	8	4	98	99
Oman	41	18	43	71
Pakistan	124	88	na	na
Panama	32	22	89	na
Paraguay	50	24	89	89
Peru	81	42	86	91

Table 3.5 Continued

	Infant mortality rate (per 1000 births)		Primary school enrolment (% of age group)	
	1980	*1996*	*1980*	*1995*
Philippines	52	37	94	100
PNG	67	62	na	na
Poland	21	12	98	97
Portugal	24	7	98	100
Romania	29	22	na	92
Russia	22	17	na	100
Rwanda	128	129	59	76
Saudi Arabia	65	22	49	62
Senegal	91	60	37	54
Sierra Leone	190	174	na	na
Singapore	12	4	99	na
South Africa	67	49	na	96
Trinidad and Tobago	35	13	90	88
Tunisia	69	30	82	97
Turkey	109	42	na	96
UAE	55	15	74	83
Uganda	116	99	39	na
UK	12	6	100	100
Uruguay	37	18	na	95
USA	13	7	95	96
Venezuela	36	22	82	88
Zambia	90	112	77	77
Zimbabwe	82	56	na	na

Source: Compiled from World Bank (*World Development Report*, various issues).

Global capital movements take on many forms. FDI flows appear less footloose and volatile compared to portfolio equity flows, generating different ramifications. The implications for developing economies have been so diverse that there exists little relationship between FDI flows, and GDP growth and improvements in material living conditions such as infant mortality rates and access to primary education. Portfolio equity and near equity capital are extremely footloose, and sites lacking effective government controls have often been subjected to volatile disruptions. The lack of institutional development in the developing economies has exposed them to extreme risks.

The lion's share of FDI flows into the developed economies and into the upper middle-income groups among the developing economies. Because the flows originate from and end in less than a quarter of the world's economies, FDI remains strongly polarized. Although national governments often support the interests of their own capital, such flows often embody considerable national interests supporting the arguments of Hirst and Thomson (1996). However, national interests also often affect capital's interests, which can be conflicting as well as complementary. In addition to facing administrative inefficiencies, governments are also influenced by bureaucrats' and politicians' interests as well as those of the electorate. International private capital functions largely to serve its directors' as well as shareholders' interests, adapting when necessary and circumventing otherwise local constraints. Where national interests contradict as well as appear insurmountable, multilateral organizations such as the WTO have become important platforms to bulldoze through asymmetric regulations. In the past, more overtly political interventions, e.g. Annaconda and Konnecott during Allende's reign in Chile, have targeted regime change.

The rising levels of portfolio equity capital in gross fixed capital formation in the developing economies have raised the degree of financial volatility. Unlike FDI where fixed physical assets and engagement in production and market contracts ensure greater permanence, portfolio equity flows can move around the world in the same day. Driven largely by sentiment, capital market investors often exit national markets abruptly when confidence levels crash. The financial rupture of a number of East Asian economies can be attributed to such withdrawals. While the problem is universal, affecting even developed economies, it has been more acute with small open economies, leaving them vulnerable to the daunting currents of the global economy.

In addition, there is no clear discernible correlation between PCI and levels of FDI participation in domestic GFCF, though the higher and middle-income economies have generally received greater FDI inflows and outflows. Even within particular regional economies, such as East and Southeast Asia, such a pattern is not observable. For example, Singapore and Malaysia show high FDI/GFCF percentages, but South Korea and Taiwan show the reverse.

However, two patterns seem obvious from the global statistics shown in the previous sections. First, the distance between the PCI of Switzerland – noted in Table 3.4 – and those of most of the rest of the economies has widened over the periods 1980–1989 and

1989–1997. Second, the distance between most developing economies and those of the mean PCIs of the developed economies has also widened in the periods 1980–1989 and 1989–1997. Obviously, the gap between the means of the PCIs of the developed economies and of the developing economies has widened.

The increased divergence, despite improvements in the material standards of some economies, reinforces many salient characteristics of capitalism identified by Marx. First, capitalist growth is contradictory and differentiating: it exacerbates the discrepancy in income levels between economies. Second, sustained GDP growth involving a number of developing economies suggests that the absolute conditions of the majority have improved over the years. Third, only a select group of economies has managed to narrow the per capita gap with the developed economies.

Two critical aspects of international private capital movements could be viewed from the foregoing discussion. The first relates to the basis behind the international movement of private capital and the second concerns the implications for growth and inequality. The evidence suggests that a wide range of factors influences private international capital movements, with most of them originating and arriving in developed economies. Although there exists no clear relationship between FDI participation levels in GFCF and PCI growth, labour-intensive and knowledge-intensive industries are concentrated in sites enjoying political stability, abundant literate labour, scarce minerals, good infrastructure, bureaucratic efficiency and in some economies, such as China and India, domestic markets. The second aspect is the absence of a significant relationship between levels of FDI participation in GFCF and GDP performance, as well as infant mortality rates and participation in basic education.

The evidence does not support the neoclassical argument that factor endowments shape the production technology of FDI. Labour-intensive firms still relocate in developing economies with a strong labour supply without adequate organization and endowed with political stability and good infrastructure. However, production has increasingly become knowledge-intensive, thereby reducing the volume of such investment in total investment. Hence, poor economies with large labour reserves and without requisite literacy levels have increasingly been bypassed by FDI. Only in sites with effective governance to meet the changing needs of capital from host governments has long-term growth been achieved. International private capital has also preferred to remain in locations where institutional support has evolved to match changes in technological requirements.

The prime exceptions to such a rule still apply to resource extraction such as oil (e.g. Saudi Arabia, Brunei and Kuwait) or agricultural cultivation such as aqua farming (Bangladesh and Indonesia).

Increased private capital movements have helped generate GDP growth in most politically stable economies. However, private international capital has generated significant spillovers only in locations such as Singapore where strong governments have contributed substantially to supporting institutional development, though failures involving bad governance have also hampered growth in many developing economies as in Indonesia. Hence, global capital movements in the absence of effective nation-states have brought little benefit to underdeveloped economies. The overall GDP trends across the globe show continued widening of PCIs. Despite increasing liberalization, the gap between the rich and poor economies has widened. Only the PCIs of eleven of the eighty-three economies reported in Table 3.4 show catching-up trends.

Stock markets have also undermined another neoclassical argument. Increased liberalization stimulated portfolio equity movements to the developing economies without adequate development of corporate governance. Massive capital movements from the mid-1980s appeared to add to the growth of the high-performing East Asian economies. However, when excessive financial exposure affected sentiments, investors suddenly withdrew their investment, causing stock markets to plummet in these economies. Only the timely intervention of the governments in Hong Kong, Singapore and Taiwan helped minimize damage to their economies. Stock and currency market ruptures and their consequent damage inflicted on the real economies in East Asia have also raised the dangers of the trend towards monopoly capital.

Conclusions

There exists little relationship between PCIs and levels of FDI participation in domestic GFCF, though more developed economies have received greater FDI inflows and outflows. Most developing economies enjoying relatively high levels of FDI participation either have strong governments promoting the conditions required by capital or are strongly endowed with natural resources. Nevertheless, these stark statements support the opening thesis of the chapter that power relations generally determine the direction of private capital flows. Foreign capital flows have been dictated by the interest of capital rather than host sites. The sheer lack of institutional development among captives and the advantages enjoyed by first-mover captors continue to make them more attractive for private capital flows. Only developing sites with natural resources, incentives, literate labour forces and political stability are sought actively by foreign capital. While only developing economies with strong economic fundamentals have managed to attract strong portfolio equity capital inflows, even these economies have been exposed to systemic disturbances. The few economies that have managed to avert serious injury (e.g. Singapore and Taiwan) did so with internal policies. The direction of FDI and portfolio equity capital supports Polanyi's contention that power relations shape capital movements.

While this chapter did not make a rigorous assessment of the impact of private capital flows on development, controlling for other variables, there appears to be little correlation between FDI participation and development. Two trends seem apparent in the relationship between FDI participation levels in GFCF and per capita GDP growth. First, the distance between the PCI of Switzerland and that of others has generally risen in the period 1980–1997. Similarly, the distance between most developing economies' PCIs and the mean PCIs of the developed economies has also widened in the period 1980–1997. Given the long time since independence, arguments that developing economies initially undergo dislocation for the initial structures to be created, or are destabilized so that imbalances for subsequent growth are generated, generally do not apply to negate these findings. The findings suggest little convergence between the developing and developed economies. Again, the pattern upholds Polanyi's (1957) contention about the relationship between power and private capital flows.

Second, general improvements in selected quality of life indicators, such as infant mortality and participation in essential education, suggest that the material conditions of the majority have advanced. Only a handful have experienced a worsening of their social circumstances in the period 1980–1996. However, a number of economies, especially those located in Africa and South Asia, remain seriously disadvantaged. Hence, while the material conditions are better, rising inequalities continue to differentiate the endowments between the poor and rich economies.

The increased divergence, despite improvements in the material standards of a number of economies, attests to some salient characteristics of capitalism. First, despite the integrating tendencies of capitalist growth, its contradictory and disembedding effects have exacerbated income differentials between economies. Second, sustained GDP growth involving a handful of developing economies suggests that the absolute conditions of the majority have elevated over the years.

Despite the euphoria surrounding the globalization process, its relationships, interactions and consequences, however sophisticated their evolution, still strongly reflect the control exerted by the powerful over the weak. While some quality of life indicators of the majority of the nations have improved, the gap between the developed and the majority of developing economies has widened. The economies with large capital resources still pervasively influence private capital movements. Some developing economies have managed to record PCI levels significantly higher than the developed economies, but they are only few in number and have remained vulnerable to the exigencies of the international economy dominated by the developed economies. The performance of the East Asian economies, which for two or three decades promised to dispel the long-held myth that developing economies are engulfed in a vicious circle of underdevelopment, is now being questioned again. East Asia's vulnerability has been seriously exposed by the financial crisis of 1997.

Liberal portfolio capital flows have also exposed small open economies to considerable risks. The dangers from stock and currency speculators who move capital swiftly across the globe have highlighted the need for effective governance. The argument that nation-states are no longer necessary in a globalized world (see Ohmae 1995) seems seriously flawed as a consequence.[7] As with the other spheres of globalization, effective governance by nation-states is critical to maximize the distribution of international private capital flows and the consequent distribution of gains to the majority.

The influence on global private capital movements seems to be dominated by a combination of decisions of capital, which is often conditioned by the environment they embed. Governments, supporting institutions and markets are extremely important when capital seeks to expand its activities to increase appropriation of profits, as well as maintain market share. Consistent with the general stance of the individual authors in this volume, the current form of globalization has forced developing national states to invent different sets of instruments to grapple with the new issues and consequences. While the improved material conditions demonstrated by most economies have driven some to liberalize more, the growing inequality between them continues to raise concerns.

While it can be argued that developing economies have faced considerable resource exploitation, it is also a fact that exploitation is the basis of accumulation. Hence, it is the extent of exploitation –

whether seriously injurious and unproductive, or progressively less injurious and productive – which is important. The development outcomes of the 1980s and 1990s suggests that the current pattern of international private capital movement is associated with the simultaneous occurrence of two conflicting processes – integration and differentiation – engendering progress in selected quality of life indicators, but at the same time widening inequalities between individual economies. Unless the growing inequalities can be reversed, the power asymmetry between individuals, nations and regions will continue to constrain the social fabric of the globe with a minority of the powerful continuing to influence unequally the destinies of the majority.

Notes

1 Comments from James Mittelman are gratefully acknowledged.
2 The topic deliberately avoided aid flows to obtain a more informed discussion of private capital movements.
3 Hirst and Thompson (1996: 2) claim that the international economy is less open and integrated than the regime that prevailed from 1870 to 1914. While the legal instruments then may have been less restrictive (e.g. in the immigration flows from Europe to North America and Australia), the increased information and material advancement of the majority and its consequent effects on the spread of knowledge raises doubts over such blanket statements.
4 See Rasiah (1996) for figures on Taiwan.
5 The regional division of labour viewed by Henderson (1990) has now taken on new dimensions following the penetration of flexible production systems in microelectronics manufacturing in Singapore, Taiwan and Malaysia.
6 For simplicity, we have avoided a test on heteroscedasticity econometrically.
7 See Gerschenkron (1962), Skocpol (1985), Amsden (1989), and Panitch (1996) for lucid arguments defending the relevance of the state in engendering and sustaining economic growth.

4 Globalization and economic disparities in East and Southeast Asia

New dilemmas

Ishak Shari

Introduction

There is increasing concern that globalization, which supports the emergence of a global market discipline as distinct from the existence of a mere global market place (Hoogvelt 1997), has worsened poverty and accentuated both national and international inequalities. In many parts of the 'Third World', burgeoning in unemployment (particularly urban unemployment), declining real wages, a growing debt burden, rising income disparities, urbanization and the feminization of poverty are some of the well-known features of the socio-economic crisis since the mid-1970s. This list could be expanded by adding new problems of drug abuse, AIDS, intensification of novel forms of violence, which seriously erode social capital – that is, the informal norms and established relationships that enable people to pursue objectives and act in concert for common benefits. Hence, despite rapid market expansion in some regions of the world, and for some segments of the workforce, the world is at the same time witnessing widening socio-economic disparities between and within countries.

Of course, there are some exceptions to this general trend. East and Southeast Asia, though increasingly integrated into the global economy, have succeeded in generating the highest sustained economic growth for any region while moving more than 370 million people out of poverty and significantly reducing income inequality. However, since mid-1997, some of these economies have experienced a drastic change in their economic and political landscape following the financial meltdown that started with the Thai baht devaluation on 2 July 1997 and rapidly spread to other countries. The ensuing economic recession has threatened to erode the remarkable achievements in reducing socio-economic disparities achieved over the thirty years before the crisis. Deep recession, especially in Indonesia, has deprived parents of the means to support their families, exposed millions of households to poverty and hunger, and even triggered sporadic ethnic and religious violence. Could the 1997–1998 'Asian crisis' signal the end of the 'Asian development model', in which the state has played a major role in national economic development? Is this recent development further evidence of what Chossudovsky (1997) described as the 'globalization of poverty', whereby evolving global structural changes have brought about the reconstitution of state institutions, the penetration of economic borders and the impoverishment of millions of people?

This chapter attempts to answer the above questions by examining the connection between liberalization and deregulation, and the pattern of poverty reduction and income inequalities in four East and Southeast Asian countries severely affected by the crisis of the late 1990s, namely Indonesia, Malaysia, South Korea and Thailand. The discussion will take into consideration the social impact of the crisis and the different responses of the government in these four countries. Based on the findings, the chapter will contest the view that globalization means the end of the state in the sense that distinct national economies and their policy strategies are increasingly irrelevant or defective. Instead, it will be argued that while some states are playing the role of promoters of the globalization process, others are authoring and resisting globalization. This will provide an alternative way of looking at the potential roles of the market, the state and civil society in achieving equitable and sustainable human development in the context of globalization.

Growth and redistribution in East and Southeast Asia

The greater integration of South Korea, Thailand, Malaysia and Indonesia into the global economy has enabled these economies to achieve rapid economic growth and significant reduction in absolute poverty and narrowing of income inequalities during the thirty years before the onset of the crisis of the late 1990s. Their exports grew at double-digit figures annually over the period 1980–1992. Of all sectors, manufacturing recorded the greatest expansion to become the most important contributor to growth in these economies. Average annual GDP growth rates exceeded 7 per cent and 6 per cent in the periods 1970–1980 and 1980–1993 respectively, resulting in a significant increase in the per capita incomes of these economies.

Unlike the experience of the United States and Western Europe, which led Kuznets to formulate the inverted 'U' curve relationship between economic growth and income inequality, South Korea, Malaysia and Indonesia apparently defied the general trend. Poverty alleviation has been a pillar of economic policy in these economies and the incidence of poverty has declined sharply in all four economies. Income inequality declined in South Korea and remained low in Indonesia over long periods. Malaysia experienced a fall in income inequality only in the period 1976–1990, while Thailand has encountered a worsening trend of income distribution over a long period.

At first glance, the experience of these economies seemed to confirm the thesis of orthodox neoclassical writers that their success was due to liberal, 'market-friendly' regimes and 'open-door' policies towards foreign trade and investment. Their experience may also be used as evidence to support the view that increased free flow of goods and capital across borders helped to accelerate convergence in living standards in the world economy. However, evidence strongly suggests that direct state intervention is a more important factor and that there exists the possibility of different trajectories of capitalist development depending on the variation in the role of the market and other institutional arrangements that act as coordinating mechanisms. Furthermore, state interventions in these economies have varied from enhancing immediate market friendliness and macroeconomic stability to deliberate efforts to promote industries with long-term objectives to speed structural change in high-productivity sectors (Amsden 1989; Wade 1990). The World Bank's *East Asian Miracle* study (1993) acknowledges several of these interventions, but asserts that only those aimed at ensuring macroeconomic stability and market friendliness were generally successful. The study contrasts the experiences of South Korea (and Taiwan) with those of the high-growth economies of Southeast Asia and maintains that interventions were extensive in the former and minimal in the latter. The World Bank study also acknowledges the distributional effects in South Korea (and Taiwan) and notes traditional practices that have brought similar results in Thailand and Indonesia, but does not recognize institutional interventions as being critical. In the case of Malaysia, the Bank's *World Development Report 1995* submitted that ethnic interventions reduced interethnic income inequalities, but increased intra-ethnic inequality so that its overall impact had not been significant (World Bank 1995: 46). Also, the latter study underlines the orthodox formula of the World Bank, which diminishes a direct allocational role for governments.

Apart from the significance of industrial policy and trade policies to promote rapid growth, these economies also implemented poverty alleviation and redistribution policies. However, the emphasis by country varied. For example, the initial boost for poverty alleviation and more equitable distribution in South Korea came through land reforms undertaken from the late 1940s. These reforms led to a reduction in land rents, the sale of public land to cultivators and tenants, and limited ownership by landowners. Low levels of concentration among food producers and US food aid under PL480 ensured affordable food prices (Hamilton 1983). Indeed, the Gini coefficient for South Korea declined slightly from 0.334 in 1965 to 0.332 in 1972 (Rao 1988; Krongkaew 1994). When food aid ceased following the 1973 oil shock, the South Korean government launched the Saemaul Undong, which, *inter alia*, stepped up domestic food supply capacity. With the help of price controls, the state succeeded in providing industrial workers with cheap food, lowering the wage bill for manufacturing firms. Price controls helped to keep consumption costs down so that the relative share of investment could rise. At the same time, control over marketing and inputs helped to protect farmers and consumers from volatile price fluctuations.

Malaysia, Thailand and Indonesia present somewhat different experiences. In particular, land reforms have not been significant in these resource-rich economies. Land in Malaysia has been distributed through land development schemes, managed by government through agencies such as the Federal Land Development Authority, the Federal Land Consolidation and Rehabilitation Authority and the Rubber Industry Smallholders Development Authority. Despite various problems, Malaysia deepened its rural development emphasis following the introduction of the New Economic Policy in 1971. Poverty reduction and ethnic distribution targets were pursued to reduce poverty incidence and achieve greater interethnic parity by the year 1990. In addition to extensive investments in developing infrastructure in rural areas where *bumiputera* (sons of the soil) were heavily concentrated, special institutions created by the government (e.g. Bank Bumiputera, Majlis Amanah Rakyat (MARA) and Pernas) were given a more direct role in uplifting the socio-economic standing of the *bumiputera*.

In Malaysia, income inequality had worsened during the early period after independence. Although the colonial government's practice of offering free education and health services, along with a progressive income tax, was continued, there were no other direct measures to alleviate poverty and inequality during the *laissez-faire* phase from independence in 1957 until 1971. The overwhelming concentration of *bumiputera* and other disadvantaged groups in rural areas obviously hampered them from gaining access to free schooling and hospitals, concentrated in urban areas. Redistributive intervention began in 1971, primarily along ethnic lines. Such redistribution involving industrial enterprises, however, began only after the promulgation of the Industrial Coordination Act in 1975 (Malaysia 1989). Thus, income inequality worsened until the mid-1970s. The Gini coefficient for income inequality rose from 0.444 in 1967 to 0.506 in 1971 and to 0.529 in 1976 (Jomo and Ishak 1986).

With the economy growing rapidly, including the boost partly attributable to export-oriented manufacturing, the poverty rate continued to decline. Also, the spread of modern farming methods in paddy cultivation – involving double cropping, green revolution strains, fertilizers, ploughing and harvesting machinery – helped to raise yields and the income levels of farmers. Other redistributive instruments, such as privileged access to education, and special support in business by MARA, Pernas and Permodalan Nasional Berhad (PNB) through, for example, captive markets and discounted loans for *bumiputera*, were also introduced. Quasi-interventions in the private sector helped push up *bumiputera* participation in the economy. Rising commodity prices and agricultural diversification to reduce dependence on particular crops helped smallholders raise household incomes in the late 1970s (Ishak 1999b, 2000). The government assumed control of rice marketing, thereby ensuring stable prices for farmers and consumers. Marketing of cash crop produce through quasi-government bodies helped smallholders reduce their dependence on unscrupulous intermediaries. The slow progress towards raising *bumiputera* share of share equity in the country's corporate sector led to new mechanisms introduced to help increase their capital–equity levels. The PNB was formed in 1978 as an additional investment arm through which the *bumiputera* trust funds, such as *Amanah Saham Nasiona* and *Amanah Saham Bumiputera*, were administered. Generous rates of dividend returns, well above market interest rates, made possible by privileged PNB investments in state-sheltered ventures (including privatized organizations), enabled the holders of such shares to enjoy substantial rents. Shares involving these trusts were actively distributed so that even the poor enjoyed relatively significant shares; poor households, farmers and labourers accounted for 49.7

per cent of the shares in 1988 (Malaysia 1991). Other redistribution efforts, as well as the expansion of more remunerative employment, especially the absorption of *bumiputera* in the public sector and wage employment in the manufacturing sector, caused income inequality to decline to 0.474 in 1984 and 0.445 in 1990 (Ishak 1999a, 1999b, 2000).

In Thailand's case, the First Economic Development Plan introduced in 1961, *inter alia*, emphasized agricultural diversification and opening up new lands (see Onchan 1997). While extensive promotion and modernization of agriculture took place, there was no significant emphasis on income redistribution to help disadvantaged groups. Hence, while food production continued to grow, enough to support the rest of the population and for export, there were no major mechanisms for redistribution. Land reforms had been formally introduced in Thailand in 1975 in the wake of the Agricultural Land Reform Act. Little real progress, however, was made, for land was transferred to influential businessmen (see Onchan 1997). Hence, despite important initiatives (including land titling services to improve property rights for landowners), land reforms were generally unsuccessful. However, growth helped lower the overall incidence of poverty, except in the mid-1980s, although income inequality continued to worsen. The government also succeeded in raising rural household incomes through the promotion of off-farm work, as in Taiwan and South Korea. As a consequence, the proportion of rural household incomes generated from off-farm activities in Thailand rose from 46 per cent in 1971–1972 to 63 per cent in 1986–1987 (Onchan 1997: 32). Off-farm activities helped reduce rural poverty in the 1985–1990 period.

Inflation management varies in these economies. The objectives of achieving rapid economic growth and price stability were accorded almost equal emphasis in Malaysia and Thailand. South Korea and Indonesia had far less control over inflation until the 1980s. Differential interest rates in the period 1950–1988 not only offered industry-subsidized credit, but also raised private savings. The average inflation rate in South Korea rose from 17.1 per cent in the 1960s to 19.5 per cent in the period 1970–1980, before falling to 6.3 per cent in the period 1980–1993 (World Bank 1995: 163). The mean inflation rate in Malaysia, Thailand and Indonesia was less than 9.0 per cent in the period 1980–1992 (World Bank 1995). While Malaysia's and Thailand's rates were low in the period 1960–1980, Indonesia faced serious inflation in the 1960s and 1970s. That South Korea and Indonesia generated far higher inflation and yet showed better income distribution in the 1960s and 1970s than in Thailand and Malaysia shows that growth and equity could be achieved so long as inflation is not extremely volatile and high (see You 1995a).

Government expenditure on social services has been crucial for ensuring the provision of minimal support for alleviating poverty, reducing inequality and sustaining growth in these economies. From the standpoint of externalities involving public goods, government participation has been vital. However, the experience of the economies under study does not suggest a positive relationship between a higher share of government expenditure on social services and the developmental position of these economies. Malaysia and Thailand show higher shares of expenditure in education and health services relative to those of South Korea over the period 1972–1993. It is also difficult to make the argument that social expenditure as a proportion of total government expenditure will fall while the country develops. Indonesia, the least developed of these economies, has shown the lowest expenditure shares in education and welfare services. However, welfare considerations – largely safety nets – show higher investment shares in South Korea, Malaysia and Thailand than in Indonesia. This evidence tends to elevate the importance of the quality of government expenditure and complementary private investments on social services.

Investments in human resources – both public and private – have also helped to reduce poverty and inequality, as exemplified in South Korea, which has a very highly educated labour force. Apart from universal primary education, even in the 1960s, South Korea had had high transition rates to secondary and tertiary levels, with emphasis on technical and engineering disciplines. The level of participation in secondary and tertiary education was similar to those of the more advanced economies.

South Korea (as well as Taiwan and Japan) deliberately advanced technical and engineering education so that the labour force was ready in the market to meet demand. Such policies helped build the market through effective interactions among the bureaucracy, firms, academia and other supply-side institutions that helped improve the anticipatory capacity of government planning. Thus, South Korea deliberately extended vocational, technical and engineering education to meet current and future demand. The state's investment in human capital went well beyond the primary stage, i.e. interventions in the labour market were based on long-term considerations beyond current prices (see Amsden 1989). The expansion of education not only helped generate technical and professional labour for industrial upgrading, but also expanded opportunities for upward social mobility, including the acquisition of skills and higher remuneration (Deyo 1989).

The emphasis on secondary and especially tertiary education in Malaysia, Thailand and Indonesia has not been comparable to that of South Korea. Hence, although basic education has offered access to low-skilled jobs in these economies, schooling has not provided as strong a means for upward social mobility for their populations. Also, while South Korea generated ample supplies of technical labour, Malaysia, Thailand and Indonesia currently face serious supply gaps for such labour; in 1990, Malaysia, Thailand and Indonesia each had 400 technologists and scientists per million people, compared to 2200 for South Korea (UNDP 1994: 17). Although Malaysia and Indonesia managed to reduce inequalities for long periods, their successes should not be misconstrued as being a result of non-interventionism, for both economies saw extensive redistributive government expenditure (see Rasiah and Ishak 1997, 1999b; Ishak 1999b, 2000).

Rapid growth, the rise in educational levels and declining unemployment have helped push up real wages in these economies despite the weakness of their trade unions. Real wages grew at an average annual rate of 10.0 per cent and 8.2 per cent respectively over the periods 1970–1980 and 1980–1992 respectively in South Korea (World Bank 1995: 175). Hence, although militancy was dealt with brutally in South Korea until democratization in the mid-1980s, efforts to promote work discipline and job enrichment through flexible human resource strategies to raise productivity (e.g. through skill intensification) helped move wages up. To improve competitiveness, the commitment to employee training – both in-firm and out-firm – has grown, thereby enhancing the versatility of labour and its skill. These developments also helped reduce occupational hierarchies and income differentials between higher and lower rung employees. Thus, when unions (including membership) began to grow stronger, real wages had already risen substantially (Deyo 1989).

From the 1970s, the growth of wage labour in Malaysia, Thailand and Indonesia intensified following rapid export-oriented manufacturing expansion, which has helped reduce disguised unemployment and raise household incomes. Wage labour grew by 8.8 per cent and 6.6 per cent per annum in Malaysia and Indonesia respectively in the 1970–1990 period. Female participation in export-oriented manufacturing expanded especially strongly in the three economies from the early 1980s (see Onchan 1997; World Bank 1993). The out-migration of rural labour to urban and industrial areas was so extensive that foreign labour had become important in low-wage modern agriculture in Malaysia in the early 1980s. Foreign labour substitution and the weakness of unions worked towards the detriment of real wage rises in plantation agriculture so that some subsectors experienced declines in real wages from the 1960s to the 1980s (see Mehmet 1986).

While export-oriented manufacturing increased the demand for labour and sparked growth in wage employment and household incomes, thus reducing poverty and income inequality, critical interventions stimulated the necessary investments. Unlike South Korea, however, industrial policy in Malaysia, Thailand and Indonesia has mitigated rapid wage rises. Thus, real wage growth has not been as substantial in Malaysia, Thailand and Indonesia. Real wages in Malaysia and Indonesia on average grew by 2.0 per cent and 5.2 per cent respectively over the period 1970–1980, and by 2.3 per cent and 4.3 per cent respectively over the period 1980–1992 (World Bank 1995: 174–175). Real wages in Thailand grew by 2.0 per cent and 2.8 per cent respectively over the periods 1973–1981, and 1981–1989 (Rasiah 1994: 210).

Besides poverty alleviation and redistribution mechanisms, the four economies have also introduced safety nets to reduce the burden of displacement created by rapid structural changes and cyclical influences. Progressive income tax, cost of living allowance (COLA) for workers, discounted housing for *bumiputera*, and low- to medium-cost housing for the underprivileged are some of the safety valves introduced in Malaysia. The effects of these instruments have, however, been mixed. The unemployed obviously cannot access COLA and access to low-cost housing schemes has been subjected to abuse by politically connected individuals.

It should be noted that South Korea was far more interventionist in the 1950s and 1960s than Malaysia and Thailand have been in recent decades. Yet, income distribution improved in the former while it worsened in the latter economies. The experience of South Korea suggests that lower inequalities are both possible and complementary to initial stages of rapid growth. They also offer a strong case for intervention to reduce poverty and improve redistribution and generate rapid growth in an increasingly globalized world. Although one may reject the South Korean experience as a special case similar to Japan and Taiwan (World Bank 1993), it is not easy to do the same with Malaysia's and Thailand's trajectories. The

Malaysian economy was largely *laissez-faire* until 1970 (World Bank 1995). Yet, its income distribution worsened continuously during this period, only to improve after interventionist redistributive policies were adopted from the 1970s. Although Thailand did not manage an effective redistribution policy, and also did not enjoy an explicitly defined industrial policy, its income Gini coefficient continued to rise. Its rural development policy, especially the promotion of off-farm work, however, successfully yielded rapid reductions in poverty, even in the mid-1980s, when urban poverty had risen. Since the 1980s, with increasing liberalization South Korea's income inequalities have begun to worsen. Similar trends appear for Malaysia following greater liberalization after the mid-1980s. These experiences seem to suggest that poverty alleviation can accompany growth, but income inequalities tend to worsen in the absence of effective redistributive interventions. However, the unique circumstances of postwar reforms (including land reforms) suggest that these initial conditions – rather than the subsequent growth process – may better explain the South Korean exception. Nonetheless, they also suggest that if such redistribution is politically feasible, it could become the basis of rapid growth, structural change and poverty alleviation.

Financial liberalization and financial crisis in Asia

While still extensively pursuing interventionist policies, all four economies have undergone considerable liberalization and deregulation in the 1980s. Much of such measures can be attributed to pressure from the major powers, particularly the United States, and international organizations such as the IMF and the World Bank, and the recognition of the feasibility of deregulation following maturization of previously protected industries. The WTO has made further liberalization virtually compulsory. South Korea, with firms at the technology frontier in several industries, appears ready to meet WTO clauses without seriously fettering their growth trends. Malaysia, Thailand and Indonesia still do not have any local firms at the technology frontier. Foreign firms – using either second- or third-generation technologies, or assembly and testing stages of production (which are technologically less sophisticated and characterized by lower value added) – are unlikely to integrate production upstream. The current promotion of high-technology industries through subsidies, including re-engineering, will be difficult to sustain with further liberalization. Technologically, catch-up industries are likely to suffer.

Apart from trade liberalization programmes, measures are undertaken to increase the space available for the private sector, by facilitating the retreat of the state wherever private enterprise is willing to play a role, under the banner of deregulation and privatization. Increasingly, the policies implemented focus on making economies more competitive internationally, through freeing of markets and curbing the role of the state, including public expenditure on social welfare, thereby having a major impact on the rural and the urban poor who may be unable to fulfil new skill requirements. In addition, since the mid-1980s, the governments in Malaysia, Thailand and Indonesia began liberalizing domestic capital markets and foreign investment regimes in their effort to foster rapid economic growth. In the 1990s, the financial liberalization process in all four economies was further accelerated. The perceived benefits from larger inflow of funds, and at a lower cost, appear to be too attractive to be ignored by the governments. At the same time, it has been argued that the four (and other Asian) governments were strongly pushed into financial opening by the US Treasury, multilateral financial institutions (particularly the IMF), as well as Wall Street fund managers, i.e. what Wade (1999) refers to as the 'Wall Street–Treasury–IMF Complex'. Consequently, large amounts of capital, particularly short-term capital, flooded into these economies.

It has been argued that one of the critical factors contributing to the financial and economic crisis in Asia in the late 1990s, seriously affecting Thailand, Indonesia, Malaysia and South Korea, was the rush for capital account liberalization without adequate prudential regulation and supervision. This move exposed these economies to great dangers of instability and crisis (see Wade 1999). In particular, after 1995, the rise of the US dollar and the depreciation of the yen and the yuan led to a loss of export competitiveness in the four economies whose currencies were pegged to the dollar. The big flow of foreign funds into these economies further exacerbated the real appreciation of the exchange rates and the loss of export competitiveness, resulting in large current account deficits, particularly in Thailand and Malaysia. The inflows of foreign funds also contributed to domestic asset bubbles, credit excesses and a growing fringe of bad investments. Hence, when the crisis hit Thailand in mid-1997, there was a violent outflow of funds from these countries. Such herd behaviour owed much to the realization that a large share of the funds should not have been committed in the first place (see Wade and Veneroso 1998).

When the financial crisis began in Thailand and then spilled over into Indonesia, Malaysia and South Korea, most analysts were expecting that it would last only some months. But the turn of events had proved them wrong. The currency and financial crisis affecting these economies has been transformed into a full-blown recession in the affected countries. In fact, the threat of currency depreciation and recession was also felt in other parts of the world, including South Africa, Russia and Brazil. Thus, it became increasingly clear that the currency crisis had developed into a financial and economic crisis, which quickly deteriorated, in turn, into a social and political crisis, affecting adversely the poor and vulnerable groups.

Even before the four countries were hit by the current financial and economic crisis, liberalization and deregulation measures appeared to affect adversely their respective income distributions. Although the overall poverty rate had continued to fall in these economies before the financial crisis, income inequality had been worsening in South Korea, Malaysia and Thailand. Increased emphasis on heavy industries and greater liberalization appear to explain rising income inequality in South Korea from the 1980s. Ownership deregulation since the mid-1980s and waning commitment to earlier redistributive mechanisms increased inequalities in Malaysia after 1990. Thailand, which has, historically, been the most liberal among the four economies, has experienced a long-term rise in income inequality. In fact, it was the only economy among the four that even recorded a rise in poverty in the mid-1980s.

The economic growth of Indonesia, Thailand, South Korea and Malaysia plunged during the crisis and even recorded negative growth for 1998. Stock market indices in all four countries fell by 30 to 50 per cent, while their currencies dropped in value by 30 to 70 per cent. The crisis in the four countries in the late 1990s is indeed unique in terms of the harshness and magnitude of its combination of problems (see ESCAP 1999).

This sudden reversal of economic growth dealt a heavy blow to employment opportunities in the affected countries. As a result, unemployment and underemployment increased significantly in these countries. In Thailand, by the third quarter of 1998, it was estimated that 250,000 workers were retrenched. The unemployment situation in Indonesia is more serious: 13.4 million people lost their jobs up to June 1998 (ESCAP 1999). In Malaysia, 83,865 workers were retrenched in 1998, compared to 18,863 during 1997 (Malaysia 1999).

Retrenchment in these countries also affected the professionals and other members of the middle class. Furthermore, the impact of the crisis on women workers, who were able to secure employment during the high-growth, pre-crisis period, seems to be more severe. In

Indonesia, for example, the textile industry, which employed mostly women, had laid off 500,000 workers by March 1998. In Thailand, by February 1998, 80 per cent of the unskilled workers laid off in the manufacturing sector were women.

Consequently, the unemployment rates in the affected countries increased significantly. In 1998, the unemployment rate in Indonesia was estimated at 10.3 per cent (compared to 4.7 per cent in 1997), 7.7 per cent in South Korea (2.6 per cent in 1997), 4.6 per cent in Thailand (1.9 per cent in 1997) and 3.9 per cent in Malaysia (2.7 per cent in 1997) (Sussangkarn *et al*. 1999: 8–9). It has been projected that a sizeable proportion of the retrenched workers may not be able to rejoin the workforce when economic growth resumes in the future. This is largely because their skill may become obsolete with the rapid restructuring of the affected economies in order to enhance their competitiveness in the world market. In addition to retrenchment and increasing underemployment, wage reductions, including non-payment of salaries, contributed to the misery in the form of reduced earnings.

The mounting retrenchment, the failure of the new entrants to the labour market to find employment, the erosion of earnings of those still employed and the rapid increase in prices brought about a sharp increase in the number of the poor in the affected countries. It was estimated, in the middle of 1998, that the poor in Indonesia swelled to 40 per cent (or 80 million out of the total population of 200 million) from 17 per cent in 1997. In Thailand and Malaysia, the poverty rate increased to 15.3 per cent and 8.0 per cent respectively in 1998 (ESCAP 1999: 121).

While the four countries are seriously affected by the financial and economic crisis, the adverse impact varies among these countries. In particular, based on the available information, it appears that the social impact of the crisis in Malaysia is relatively less severe than it is in the other three countries. One explanation for this is the different ways the governments responded to the unprecedented financial and economic turmoil. Thailand, South Korea and Indonesia sought IMF assistance while Malaysia refused it. IMF intervention, however, required the governments in the three countries to cut domestic expenditures and raise interest rates to high levels through fiscal and monetary tightening measures. These policy adjustments led to further contraction of the economies and worsening of the social impact of the crisis. In addition, the IMF required substantial reforms in areas such as corporate governance, labour markets and trade regimes.

Malaysia, on the other hand, introduced selective capital control on 1 September 1998 to insulate the economy from externally generated risks and vulnerabilities. The new Malaysian policy package included: (a) the official fixing of the ringgit at RM3.80 to the US dollar (though the ringgit value in relation to other currencies will still fluctuate according to their own rates against the dollar); (b) measures to eliminate the international trade in the ringgit by bringing back to the country ringgit-denominated financial assets, such as cash and savings deposits via the non-recognition or non-acceptance of such assets in the country after a one-month deadline; (c) the stipulation that non-residents purchasing local shares will not be able to withdraw from the country the proceeds from the sale of the shares for a year from the purchase date; (d) all dealings in shares listed on the Kuala Lumpur Stock Exchange (KLSE) must be affected through the exchange or a stock exchange recognized by the KLSE; (e) measures curbing the taking out or bringing in of funds by Malaysians travelling abroad are limited to carrying RM1000 and to another RM10,000 worth of foreign currency while non-resident travellers can take out foreign currencies up to the amount they brought in (and no limit on import of foreign currencies); and (f) imposing conditions on the operations and transfers of funds in external accounts. Foreign direct investors, who are free to repatriate their earnings, are not affected as these controls are aimed at containing the impact of short-term fund flows.

The long-term impact of Malaysia's capital control is still uncertain though there are criticisms that the measure was too late because most funds had moved out of the country and that it is ill-timed and was unnecessary as the market panic against Asian economies began to subside. Nevertheless, the short-term macroeconomic impact of the measures seems to be favourable in lessening the adverse impact of the crisis. With the introduction of the selective capital control measures, the monetary authority in Malaysia was able to reduce the interest rate sharply and to grant firms access to cheaper loans so as to avoid bankruptcy, thus reversing the negative impact of earlier measures of tight monetary and fiscal policy. The easing of monetary policy was accomplished without triggering currency depreciation, thus resolving the policy dilemma of lowering the interest rate while maintaining a stable currency. At the same time, the selective capital control has also enabled the government to adopt an expansionary fiscal policy.

Conclusion

The consequences of globalization and liberalization for growth, poverty and income inequality in East and Southeast Asia are quite complicated and contingent. Available information does not allow a full-blown assessment of the welfare consequences of recent globalization and liberalization for different socio-economic groups, including the poor and vulnerable groups. Furthermore, while some analysts are quick to jump to the conclusion that the crisis has proven the failure of the 'Asian development model', the discussion above has shown that the issue is more complex. While it must be admitted that the crisis has demonstrated the truth of the allegation that this model encourages corruption and nepotism, particularly in the case of Indonesia, there may be a larger truth that still needs to be discovered. In this context, the following quotation from Stiglitz (1999: 3) is worth considering:

> Some ideologues have taken advantage of the current problems besetting East Asia to suggest that the system of active state intervention is the root of the problem ... But I will argue that the heart of the current problem in most cases is not that government has done too much, but it has done too little ...
>
> The East Asian crisis is not a refutation of the East Asian miracle. The more dogmatic version of the Washington Consensus does not provide the right framework for understanding both the success of the East Asian economies and their current troubles. Responses to East Asia's crisis grounded in this view of the world are likely to be, at best badly flawed, and at worst counterproductive.

The IMF and the World Bank have long advocated the liberalization of capital markets, largely ignoring the arguments for financial repression and restraint, and the fact that there is no guarantee the market-determined outcome will be efficient, socially optimal, or even stable as information in the financial market is costly and asymmetric (World Bank 1999). There is also a significant body of persuasive contrarian literature (e.g. Singh 1995) which raises serious doubts about the nature and contribution of equity financing to late industrialization. The 1997–1998 crisis dealt a major setback to the international financial institutions' stance on financial liberalization. The Asian experience shows that unregulated finance capital will end up largely in short-term and speculative ventures, which will in the long run debilitate growth and efforts to eradicate poverty and reduce income inequalities. Consequently, there is now greater appreciation among governments of the dangers of exposing their financial systems to fast liberalization, especially when they lack experience in dealing with the international capital market and when their banking regulation and supervision are in need of upgrading. Governments are now more willing to discipline not only labour but also finance.

The above discussion also challenges the common assertions that with globalization, the state is increasingly irrelevant (Ohmae 1991) or that the power of the state is being transcended and is increasingly becoming hollow and defective (Strange 1995). The developments in East and Southeast Asia demonstrate the possibility of different trajectories, despite being increasingly integrated in the globalized world economy, due to variation in the role of markets and the state as coordinating mechanisms – hence, the stress on the importance of a stronger role of the state in developing countries in order to promote equitable and sustainable human development during the present phase of globalization. This argument, however, does not ignore two convincing arguments against the state, namely: (a) the propensity and capacity of the state for authoritarian repression not only of people but also of institutions, social practices and the very fabric of everyday life; and (b) its inefficiency as an economic actor.

However, the experience of the financial crisis of the late 1990s in Thailand, Malaysia, Indonesia and South Korea demonstrates that the implementation of the neoliberal version of globalization, particularly financial liberalization, has brought about widespread hardship among the disadvantaged groups in the affected countries, causing political and social turmoil. Policy prescriptions from the IMF, which involved tight monetary and fiscal policies, worsened the suffering of those adversely affected by the crisis. The aims of IMF policies appeared to ensure the maintenance of the domestic currency's convertibility and free capital flows, and guaranteeing repayment of foreign lenders. According to UNCTAD's *Trade and Development Report 1998* (1998c), the foreign lenders emerged from the crisis without substantial loss even though they had accepted exposure to risk just as other lenders had done.

Therefore, in a world in which powerful international organizations and transnational corporations as well as the states in the advanced industrial countries are devoted to maximizing the freedom of financial capital around the globe, and in the absence of any new international financial architecture, the states in developing countries need to assert social control and to continue to pursue redistributive policies that could change the impact of the globalization process on their people. In this regard, however, a fundamentally different alternative, involving the democratization of the state and the economy, would have to be considered. This would require a challenge to the national and international structures of power. In this regard, Higgott's proposal for an alternative is worthy of further consideration:

> We may be seeing a trend away from 'automatic pilot' types of market strategy towards more active policies of the types enshrined in the Asian 'development state' model ... [The] impact of the global economic crisis has created a space for the opinion that there are more than the traditional two economic policy agendas available to governments. A third way would involve some sort of 'middle' ground; in which the regulatory role of governments might be revitalized, greater attention might be given to social issues, and the emergence of a more 'national' or possibly post-crisis 'regional' approaches to economic management might be facilitated.
>
> (Higgott 1999: 12–13)

5 Globalization and democratization

The response of the indigenous peoples of Sarawak

Sabihah Osman

Introduction

Globalization is a multilayered and dialectical process involving both homogenization and particularization, i.e. the rise of localism in politics, economics, religion and culture. In what ways do these contending forces operate in Sarawak and in Malaysia as a whole? This chapter examines how globalization impacts on the democratization process and other political activities of the indigenous peoples (IPs) of Sarawak and shows how the democratization process is a force in capturing globalization.

Impact of globalization on democratization

Sarawak is one of the states in the Federation of Malaysia. Situated in the western region of the Island of Borneo and with a total area of about 724,450 square miles (1,876,325 square kilometres), Sarawak is almost as large as the whole of Peninsular Malaysia.

The population of Sarawak consists of several IPs, such as Iban, Bidayuh, Malays, Melanau, Kayan and Kenyah. Unlike Peninsular Malaysia, where the population is made up of approximately 55 per cent Malays, 34 per cent Chinese, and 11 per cent Indians and others, no single ethnic group in Sarawak is dominant. In 1998, the Sarawak population numbered 1.99 million, consisting of 5.6 per cent Melanau, 21.4 per cent Malays, 28.6 per cent Iban, 8 per cent Bidayuh, 6 per cent other indigenous people, 27 per cent Chinese, 3.9 per cent others, including non-Malaysian citizens (Department of Statistics Malaysia 1998). Hence, unlike Peninsular Malaysia, Sarawak politics and political alignments have been relatively fluid because no one ethnic group has a clear majority; each group must manoeuvre to seek the support of others (Leigh 1974).

As in the other states of Malaysia, the concept of democracy and multiparty elections is not entirely new to Sarawak. In 1956, elections were held for the Kuching Municipal Council. Subsequently in 1963, the first general elections based on the three-tier voting system were organized (Porritt 1997: 23–24, 27). It was, however, in June 1970 that the first direct elections were conducted and resulted in no single party garnering majority support. The formation of a new state government, therefore, was beset with problems. As a result, a coalition government based on consociational politics was set up when the Sarawak United People's Party (SUPP) joined the coalition and established a new government led by Parti Bumiputera (Sanib 1985: 124–125). With this coalition, Sarawak entered the 1970s with the Malay-Muslims playing an important role in the state government until the present. The Sarawak state government has been based on a 'grand coalition' to ensure political stability and to generate economic growth.

However, political party formation and elections are only part of the democratic process. The popular phraseology that democracy is 'government of the people, for the people, by the people', is too formalistic, often associated with the US form of government. Western liberal democracy within a capitalist economy focuses on individual liberties. To the liberals, 'the ballot box [is] the mechanism whereby the individual citizens as a whole periodically confer authority on government to enact laws and regulate economic and social life' (Held 1995: 17–18).

Nevertheless, Malaysian democracy is 'neither unambiguously democratic nor authoritarian' (Crouch 1996); it has also been described as 'a semi-democracy or a democratic-authoritarian state' (Case 1993, 1997). The government is elected through voting once every five years at both state and federal levels. As citizens in a democratic state, the people are aware of their rights and obligations, although some tend to view the system as something imposed from above. This is evident from a survey conducted in Sarawak in September 1996.[1] The results of the survey indicate that the IPs are aware of the meaning of democracy, which is not only about holding elections, but also about allowing all views, particularly from the grassroots, to be heard and dissent to be voiced. For example, during the 1996 Sarawak state election campaigns, voters consistently raised issues related to land, logging, social justice, and the Bakun dam project and its impact on the IPs in the Sungai Balui Valley.

Within this framework, one can pose questions about whether the democratic process has enriched some, but disadvantaged others. To what extent have the IPs aligned themselves with the system? Has the tide of globalization exerted pressure towards greater political, social and cultural democratization in Sarawak? In addition, is democracy perceived differently at various levels of representation? Besides holding and participating in elections, at the grassroots level, democracy revolves around the question of freedom of expression, freedom of the press and freedom for the local people to exercise their rights, e.g. to maintain a sustainable environment and the right to customary land.

This, however, does not mean that non-Western states are strangers to democracy, and democracy appears in various forms depending on the socio-economic and cultural milieu of the society in question (Mittelman 1996a: 8; Held 1991: 139–172). In Malaysia, including Sarawak, democracy as an idea and practice has been expressed in the form of *musyawarah*, i.e. consensus in decision making, which has long been a salient feature of the indigenous political system. The appointment of village heads and *tuai rumah* (longhouse headman) illustrates this.[2]

Although political parties and regular elections are recent phenomena, the idea and process of democracy are part and parcel of the indigenous communities and have been entrenched in their value systems. Amongst the IPs, the democratic processes have long been practised even in the remote areas, e.g. *musyawarah*. The IPs fully understand their democratic rights in terms of land rights and environmental issues, and what they are fighting for. Regarding logging activities and the resistance to it, Along Sega' a Penan from Ulu Limbang affirmed his rights when he said:

> The earth is like our mother, our father. If you from the government give orders to the companies to invade our land, you might as well cut off our heads and our parents' heads too. When the bulldozers tear open the earth, you can see her blood and her bones even though she can't speak ... The forest is our home, our pantry, our department store and hospital. Whether we are bitten by snake, or suffering from a headache, a fever or an injury, our doctor has always been there for us ... We always know how to get food in our undisturbed land and we aren't dependent on your hand-outs ... Our land is not so large ... We are in trouble because our land has been taken and we have been made poor ... The fish in the river die because of the polluted water. The game flee because of the companies (timber companies). Why doesn't the government discuss it and educate people about it? Our

Chief Minister, Taib Mahmud, should revoke the timber licenses. Why won't he help us? If we don't blockade, who is going to listen to us? That's why I blockade. But Taib Mahmud shouldn't send the police and lay charges against us! It would be good if the Prime Minister would come to see me for himself!

(Manser 1996: 46–49)

Along Sega''s grievances were shared by his fellow countryman, Saya' Megut. In his message to Sarawak's Chief Minister Taib Mahmud, Saya' wrote:

what kind of a government is ours? Can this be considered a government when the people have no right to live on their traditional lands? The companies are pushing ever further into the interior. What is behind it? The government! Does it want to destroy the entire land so it can say 'That's where we have established a reservation for the Penans?' ... We are tired of hearing the bulldozers which are penetrating our land. Our land is no longer the black edge of a fingernail. We have no other land.

(Manser 1996: 215)

Subsequently, on 22 August 1995, a group of thirteen Penan from Ulu Baram signed a declaration which stated:

Although the government demanded that we become settled, we have been ignored. Even our fields have been run over by bulldozers ... We ask all our 'relatives', wherever you are, for help. Speak forcefully with our government so that it stops the companies and places our communal areas in Ulu Baram under protection.

(Manser 1996: 215)

Hydroelectric dam project

The IPs' commitment to maintain their democratic rights can be seen in their struggle to protect the environment. Concern about environmental impact has surfaced because a decade ago the Sarawak government forced the Iban of Batang Ai to resettle in a new area, because their longhouses were situated at the site of the proposed hydroelectric dam, supposed to be the first hydroelectric power dam in the state. The Batang Ai dam is situated in the Lubok Antu District in Sri Aman Division. It was completed and officially opened in August 1985. The people affected by the Batang Ai dam project were predominantly Iban. The Iban are not a landless people; they, in fact, own large tracts of land held under native customary rights. The dam project involved the resettlement of twenty-nine longhouses above the dam and four longhouses below the dam site. The project has unquestionably brought some advantages, for each family in the resettlement scheme was given 11 acres (4.5 hectares) of land, 5 for rubber cultivation, 3 for cocoa, 2 for paddy or general farming land and 1 for orchards. But the disadvantages seem to outweigh the positive impact. For example, there have been problems with loan repayments and the rapid depletion of the compensation paid. But the most important issue has been the erosion of the cultural identity of the Iban in Batang Ai (Jayum A Jawan 1994: 201–203; INSAN and authors 1992). According to John Phoa:

> Resettlement from dam projects has meant a huge [*sic*] loss of customary tenure to the native lands. They also lost their ancestral land and customary rights, as well as sacred burial ground and the forest which have been a major source of their subsistence. The forest and customary rights are part and parcel of the traditional and *adat* (customary law) of the shifting cultivators. Such losses are often accompanied by the break-down of the social fabric of the indigenous peoples.
>
> (Phoa 1996: 211)

With regard to cultural aspects, we have to take into account the worldview of the IPs. In general, the economy of the IPs is small scale; their life is associated with their land from which they derive their food and develop their culture. However, landownership varies from one ethnic group to another. The Iban and Penan, for instance, are basically non-hierarchical though there is some differentiation based on gender and age. Although essentially egalitarian, the Iban have been aware of long-standing status distinctions among themselves of *raja berani* (wealthy and brave), *mensia seribu* (commoners) and *ulun* (slaves), with prestige still accruing to descendants of the first status and disdain to descendants of the third. The Brooke dynasty, which ruled Sarawak from 1841 to 1941, created political positions – headman (*tuai rumah*), regional chief (*penghulu*) and paramount chief (*temenggong*) – in order to restructure Iban society for administrative control, especially for taxation and the suppression of head-hunting (Sutlive 1992: 8). In the case of the Penan, they know no hierarchy because they live in very small and independent groups; they have no need of chiefs and representatives (Manser 1996: 26). The Kelabit, Kenyah, Kayan and Melanau practise a hier-archical social structure (King 1990).

The IPs' respect for their land permits them to conserve their ecosystems for long-term use. Conservation, however, is in conflict with the Malaysian government in general and the Sarawak govern-ment in particular, which, under globalization, seeks the integration of the economy into the open and free-market system (Maiguashca 1994: 368). As we shall see below, the IPs become major victims of the policies that have been pushed by the globalization strategy. Market-led developments such as logging and hydroelectric power dams affect their economic system and their traditional livelihood. This is evident among the IPs from the Asia Pacific Economic Co-operation (APEC) countries. Supported by various non-governmental organizations (NGOs), their worsening plight has been highlighted in the mass media.

During the three APEC summit meetings in 1995, 1996 and 1998, NGOs have held their own parallel gatherings (Gaspar 1997: 106), later known as the Asia Pacific Peoples' Assembly (APPA). APPA is an annual forum which highlights concerns about the 'free trade, free market' model of trade and investment liberalization that APEC promotes. APPA seeks to resist globalization and to change its agenda. At a forum on 'Confronting Globalization: Reasserting Peoples' Rights', APPA participants reviewed the effects of globaliza-tion on specific areas, including land, food security and agriculture, labour migrants workers, women, the environment and forestry, human rights and democracy, privatization and financial deregula-tion, and youth and education. APPA considers globalization to be a process that concentrates capital and political control in the hands of a select few, rather than distributes them equitably among the masses. Globalization also contains economic and social contradic-tions, and countries with different levels of development are not treated as equals. As a result, developed nations are in a better posi-tion to exploit developing ones. Thus, the sustainable development agenda that emerged within APEC in 1993 is perceived as mere rhetoric. It cannot be denied that globalization, which thrives on the promotion of an ideology of consumerism and individualism, has accelerated environmental abuse the world over, intensifying the destruction of various ecosystems. At the same time, globalization has helped enhance rights consciousness and democratic impulses in significant ways. APPA has affirmed that 'What we need is true democratic cooperation among peoples and countries of the

Asia-Pacific based on equality and mutual benefit, and upholding the realisation of the peoples' sovereignty and self-determination' (as quoted in *The Sunday Magazine* 13 December 1998).

While not supportive of the idea of a free-trade area, Malaysia's Prime Minister Mahathir Mohamad sees APEC as being able to contribute to the well-being of its members. He also believes that there could be 'social and political spin-offs from the APEC process … which should be regarded as a bonus' (Gaspar 1997: 75). Thus, in order to achieve the main goal and its bonus, the Malaysian state and big business give priority to the push for economic growth at the expense of the IPs and the environment. As such, Malaysia's logging companies continue to export raw hardwood and cut timber, leading to destructive deforestation. As shown in Sarawak, the IPs have been the most affected by the disappearance of the forests in areas where their native customary rights are supposed to be constitutionally guaranteed.

Indigenous movements throughout the world have begun to realize their rights and have demanded their special claims to the land (Maiguashca 1994: 370). These movements have to some degree created uneasiness in Malaysia. Despite their differences, the IPs, however, are eager to be part of the ongoing development. 'They look forward to a good life, a stable family, a peaceful community life and want to cultivate cordial relations with other groups in the larger national community … They want their self-pride and dignity to be respected and safeguarded' (Hassan 1998: 3).

In 1997, the IPs were displaced for the second time in order to enable the Malaysian government to build the Bakun dam. Upon completion, the 2400 megawatt hydroelectric power project will transmit electricity by underwater cables not only within Malaysia, but also to a few neighbouring Southeast Asian countries. Since this RM13.5 billion[3] grandiose project has a great impact on the environment, the IPs who live around the proposed project and the environmentalists have made a number of protests. However, the government ignores their resistance. In fact, in the beginning, the project was sold to Ekran Bhd, owned by a Sarawakian timber tycoon/hotel builder. Because of the 1997–1998 economic and currency crisis, the federal government took over the project, which has now been postponed indefinitely. Nevertheless, resettlement of the affected 10,000 IPs residing in the reservoir zone had not, in the same way, been postponed.

The prime minister's announcement of the project's 'indefinite postponement' on September 1997 was regarded as a triumphant vindication for the project's 'many opponents'. These opponents always asserted that the mega project would be a 'major economic disaster', quite apart from its 'socially and environmentally destructive impact' (Salleh 1999). Since 'it poses grave threats to the economy, ecology and the livelihood of the affected indigenous people', the Coalition of Concerned Non-Governmental Organizations on Bakun, which comprises forty NGOs, argued that the project should be scrapped. On 8 June 1999, the prime minister announced that the government was going ahead with the Bakun project and Tenaga Nasional Berhad will play the leading role when the stalled project resumes (*The Sun* 9 June 1999). However, the power generation capacity of the dam will be scaled down to 500 megawatts, although there is 'a possibility of a higher figure'. The government promises to pay a total of RM950 million to take over from Ekran Bhd and other parties. The estimated cost will be about RM5 billion to complete the project. According to the prime minister, the government wanted to complete the project as soon as possible because of the rising demand for electricity following economic recovery.

Much of the energy produced by the scaled-down Bakun dam project would have to be consumed in Sarawak itself, because the government plans to site energy-intensive industries in Sabah and Sarawak. The question is, will investors bring energy-intensive industries there? (*The Sun* 9 June 1999). This is unlikely, as Sarawak has spare capacity beyond its present and foreseeable future needs (Jomo 1999). The Deputy Chief Minister of Sarawak, George Chan, disclosed that Sarawak has excess capacity and does not need any more power. At the federal level the Deputy Energy Minister, Chan Kong Choy, was reported as having said that 'our reserve power supply of 45 per cent will be able to meet the nation's needs until the year 2000'. In fact, Chan stressed that the new plants in Perlis, Perak and Kedah will provide about 3000 megawatts (about 25 per cent more) than the power expected to be generated by the proposed Bakun dam (Jomo 1999)

To make way for the construction of the Bakun dam, a group of Badǝng (the subgroup of the Kenyah community) which have been residing in Long Geng settlement and Long Bulan are amongst the 10,000 IPs who have to be resettled. For the villagers, the question of resettlement is the main focus in regard to the Bakun project. They understood that despite their protest against the project which might result in flooding their area, including many of their ancestors' graveyards, there is no alternative. So far they have avoided radical confrontation with the state. The strategy has been for the affected villagers to link up with NGOs to tell the world that they oppose the Bakun dam project, which will flood their homeland. To make the most out of the project, they wanted guarantees from the government that basic facilities such as clinics and schools would be made available as well as easy access to towns so that they could sell their farm products (Tan Chee Beng 1997: 164).

Although the downsized Bakun dam project would be postponed, the resettlement of the indigenous dwellers living in the reservoir zone was to be implemented as previously scheduled. In fact, as stated by a fact finding mission sent by the Coalition of Concerned NGOs on Bakun to Sarawak, the authorities there were 'rushing the resettlement' process; they wanted 'Operation Exodus' to be completed by August 1999, despite the downsizing of the power generation capacity of the dam (*Harakah* 14 June 1999).

It is thus clear that large-scale government development programmes have threatened the IPs. Their land is taken away in the name of development for the benefit of a few. Development activities such as hydroelectric dams, plantations, or tourism projects uproot and forcefully displace the IPs. Furthermore, since mid-1995, the Sarawak government has been promoting the New Concept of Native Customary Land Development for large-scale oil palm plantations. Under this concept, the native customary lands will be leased out to private plantation company developers for a period of sixty to ninety years. As a result, the IPs will most likely lose the rights to their land. Some of the IPs oppose this kind of development, which will rob them of their customary land.

Logging activities

Besides the Bakun and Batang Ai dam projects, the problem of logging also faces the IPs. Logging operations may not only cause ecological disaster but also affect the economy and health of the IPs.

> In the hilly terrain, logging reduced the water-holding capacity of the land, affecting many plant and animal species and destroying the food web. The IP's major source of protein, namely the wildlife and fish life in the forests and its waters, was severely depleted.
>
> (INSAN and authors 1992: 17, 61, 65–67)

The increased logging activities have also attracted the attention of environmentalists. As a result, the local population has become more conscious of environmental repercussions and of problems arising from logging, for they are the ones living closest to the forest and, therefore, are most threatened by the reckless destruction of their habitat.

Timber has been Malaysia's second-largest export earner after petroleum since the early 1980s. In 1990, export earnings from timber and timber products amounted to RM8.9 billion – or 11.3 per cent of total export proceeds – compared to RM10.6 billion for petroleum, RM4.4 billion for palm oil and RM3.0 billion for rubber (INSAN and authors 1992: 1). Although by the end of the 1970s diminishing available forest resources and heightened public awareness of their grave environmental consequences had reduced logging in Peninsular Malaysia, timber production in both Sarawak and Sabah had nevertheless increased. By 1990, Sarawak accounted for 18.8 million, or 47 per cent, of the 40 million cubic metres logged in Malaysia. At this rate, an average of 1850 acres (750 hectares) are being taken out from Sarawak every day (INSAN and authors 1992: III). The main buyers are Japan, taking 45 per cent of the total, and Taiwan, 20 per cent. Timber is mainly exported to the European Economic Community (EEC) (Phoa 1996: 201) and timber concessionary rights have become a coveted prize for political office and power, engendering a vicious cycle of timber politics. Hence, the political economy of timber has shaped and moved Sarawak politics, at least over the last two decades. The question is, who benefits from the timber activities? As pointed out by Edmund Langgu in Parliament, 'It would appear that after years of accelerated timber exploitation, very few rural dwellers have benefited directly except as labourers' (INSAN and authors 1992: 17).

The Sarawak Study Group's pioneering research on logging in Belaga notes that political power and family connections with leading state government politicians primarily determine access to timber concessions. Another set of beneficiaries is the logging operators – urban ethnic Chinese Sarawakians – who actually run the timber extraction and export activities (INSAN and authors 1992: VII).

Besides logging activities, the environmentalists have also highlighted issues such as illegal logging,[4] favouritism in granting logging concessions and corruption. Moreover, those who benefit most are the state government, concessionaires, timber contractors and subcontractors. The timber workers, the majority of whom are the IPs, account for less than 4 per cent of recipients of the total gross income earned from the sale of timber, although they make up more than 95 per cent of the total population of those involved in the industry. It cannot be denied that, on the one level, timber activities helped Sarawak to develop, but for the population as a whole, the problems outweigh the advantages (Hurst 1990: 91).

In response to criticism from the environmentalist movements, the governments accuse them of trying to cut off a growth-based economy at its early stages of development. They 'would deny poorer countries their best prospects of escape from the poverty trap' (Hurst 1990: 482). Therefore, some states are reluctant to facilitate coordination by establishing effective global governance mechanisms in relation to the environmental agenda.

The Malaysian Premier Dr Mahathir Mohamad said, 'the timber industry helps hundreds of thousands of poor people in Malaysia ... we don't cut all trees when we do logging in the forests. Only marked mature trees are cut. We also do reforestation' (as quoted in INSAN and authors 1992: 2–74). He went on to say that 'Malaysia is a poor country and just developing, and it is important for it to earn a little revenue from its rich forest resources' (as quoted in Manser 1996: 272). His views have been echoed by the Sarawak Chief Minister, Taib Mahmud, who claimed that

> the timber industry has helped to pull out more than half of those trapped in the poverty level [*sic*]. We develop big timber operations which would yield [*sic*] thousands of miles of roads and hundreds of bridges and at the same time provide jobs for the local people on a more secure and continued basis.
>
> (As quoted in Manser 1996: 205)

James Wong, Sarawak's Minister of Environment and Tourism, who himself controls over 650,000 acres (263,250 hectares) of forest concessions even argued that 'This land does not belong to the natives. It is state land' (INSAN and authors 1992: 82). Yet the International Mission on 'Natives' Rights and Rainforests found evidence that Wong's own timber business, namely Limbang Trading Company Limited, one of the country's most prosperous timber companies, sells timber from the protected species list of the government's Select Committee on Fauna and Flora (INSAN and authors 1992: 82).

The lucrative nature of the timber industry helps to explain why the state government became more defensive and sometimes easily repealed its constitutional obligations to the IPs by ignoring their rights to customary land when it was challenged by protests and blockades from the indigenous communities. These protests and blockades are an exercise by the IPs in defence of their democratic rights. In October 1987, the Malaysian government took a harsh measure by detaining forty-two IPs in Uma Bawang on charges of 'wrongful restraint' because they refused to dismantle their blockades and 'unlawful occupation of state lands'. The IPs had been engaged in a seven-month blockade to halt the logging of their ancestral lands. The arrests were made following a major series of arrests in Peninsular Malaysia. Among those detained under the Internal Security Act (ISA) was Harrisson Ngau, a Kayan and a social activist.[5] With the blockades of timber roads and with other kinds of resistance to forest destruction in Sarawak, international and Malaysian attention have been focused on the problem of logging and other environmental issues in Sarawak and Malaysia. However, these incidents prompted the Sarawak State Legislative Assembly to amend the Forest Ordinance on 25 November 1987, making it punishable by a two-year jail term and a fine of $6000 if a person sets up a structure on a road constructed by a timber licensee or a permit holder. As a result, in December 1987, forty-one Penan and Kayan and two members of Friends of the Earth Malaysia were imprisoned. However, this arrest did not stop a group of Penan representatives from declaring that the amendment is unjust and reaffirming their right to blockade on their own land to protect it.

The blockades were followed by a series of protests and blockades in other areas, such as in Sungai Tatau, Bintulu, in 1989, Long Geng Village in the upper Rejang River in 1990 and in Belaga District in July 1991. For the Tatau case, eight Iban launched a blockade to prevent the timber company, Daiya Malaysia Sdn. Bhd. from encroaching further on native customary land. In the case of Long Geng Village, eight Kenyah set up a human blockade to stop the logging activities in that area. As a result of the Tattoo blockade, eight Ban were sentenced to prison terms between six and nine months, after being found guilty to the charge of 'criminal intimidation'. Eight Kenyah from the Long Geeing Village were forced to sign a bond of good behaviour for six months and were later released (Phoa 1996: 204). In August 1991, eight Ban were sent to prison following a series of protests involving more than seventy men, women and children in an attempt to protect their customary land rights from encroachment by a logging company, Hua Seng Sawmill Sdn. Bhd. (Phoa 1996: 204; Gaspar 1997: 76–80). In Kanowit, another blockade occurred at Long Ajeng, Baram, where a group of Penan, with the support of other indigenous communities, organized a protest to prevent the logging of the area to which the Penan people claim customary rights. Besides arresting and charging the indigenous groups concerned, the state government also charged the individual protesters, including a local environmentalist, Anderson Mutang Urud, a Kelabit, leader of the Sarawak Indigenous People's Alliance (SIPA) from Long Napir in Ulu Limbang. He was charged under Section 42 of the Societies Act for alleged involvement in an illegal society and provoking unrest in February 1992.

In response to the IPs' struggle and protest movements, the state government accused green activists, such as Friends of the Earth Malaysia, the Greenpeace movement in Germany, and individuals such as Bruno Manser from Switzerland, of instigating the IPs in launching their protests and blockades. Commenting on this particular 'interference', Sarawak Chief Minister Taib Mahmud said, 'It is our hope that outsiders will not interfere in our internal affairs, especially people like Bruno Manser. The state government of Sarawak has nothing to hide. Ours is an open liberal society' (*Borneo Bulletin* 19 July 1987, as quoted in Manser 1996: 160). To counter the allegations and criticisms, the state government tightened control over the entry of foreign environmentalists, journalists and film crews into the state. As pointed out by the Sarawak chief minister, foreign environmental activists 'have no right to come and stir up trouble in the State' (*New Straits Times* 8 July 1991). At the same time, the government blacklisted individuals from foreign countries and Peninsular Malaysia, particularly Friends of the Earth Malaysia and Bruno Manser, from entering the state. The state government defended its timber policy on the grounds that

> Sarawak was heavily dependent on its logging industry to progress. Logging not only brought in revenues of several billion ringgit a year to the State in terms of export profits, it also generated business opportunities throughout the State. And it helped to feed more than 250,000 men, women and children of the State's population.
>
> (Ritchie 1993: 61)

In support of the state government, the Malaysian government has engaged foreign researchers to counter what it regards as misrepresented reports about Malaysian logging activities in 1992. The project, which cost between RM5 and RM10 million, focused on the socio-environmental aspects of the timber industry with special reference to Sarawak and was sponsored by the Malaysian Timber Industry Development Council and the Sarawak Timber Industry Development Corporation (Phoa 1996: 208).

Although the response from the state and the federal government as regards the IPs' blockades and protest movements was to a certain extent negative, it nevertheless managed to attract international and Malaysian attention to the problem of logging in Sarawak. Overall, the globalization process has made it possible for the IPs to build up networks with other NGOs in and outside the country. A number of people's organizations have arisen among the IPs such as Uma Bawang Residents' Association in Sarawak, Sarawak Penan Association, SIPA, Friends of the Earth Malaysia, with bases in Sarawak and the Borneo Resources Institute (BRIMAS), an NGO which works on indigenous issues and acts as a research and resource centre on such issues. The protest movements, thus, should be seen in the wider context of globalization. They manifest the IPs' struggle in defence of environmental rights and social justice – 'in other words, about a just state' (Fadzilah Majid-Cooke 1999), and about a just social order for actors involved at various political levels, including non-state politics. Although the protest movements were easily quashed, the real grievances and deep-seated resentments persist.

Concluding remarks

In the above discussion, we have looked at the impact of globalization on democratization and how globalization forces have disrupted the IPs' everyday life by such process as logging activities and hydroelectric dam projects.

Sarawak has benefited considerably from socio-economic development, but uneven development and marginalization of certain groups, particularly the IPs, are also a reality. As mentioned, the integration of Sarawak's economy into a more open and free-market system has affected the IPs' everyday lives. Through the state or private development activities, such as land development, changes in agricultural activities, logging, road building, the expansion of urban areas and the development of hydroelectric power like the Bakun dam project, the IPs of Sarawak have been forcefully displaced and relocated to new areas.

The destruction of the tropical rainforest by logging activities in Sarawak, in fact, is not limited to local controversial issues such as blockades and unlawful occupation of state land between the IPs of Sarawak and the governments of Malaysia and Sarawak. As noted, in some situations, the federal and state governments have treated this problem as a serious global issue between the international NGOs and the governments of Malaysia and Sarawak. In this instance, globalization has affected both the nation-state and the IPs in different ways.

In the case of Sarawak, globalization has triggered greater awareness among the IPs of self-empowerment and democratization, which are important forces in capturing globalization. The IPs of Sarawak have been more courageous and bolder than their counterparts in Peninsular Malaysia. Through their blockades and protest movements, they have shown that they know how to use 'power' to speak and to resist the globalizing forces that threaten their lifestyles and economic activities.

Notes

1 The research was conducted in Kuching, Samarahan, Asajaya and Simunjan. The research team consisted of Rashila Ramli, Bilcher Bala and Sabihah Osman, all of Universiti Kebangsaan Malaysia, and Lim Phay Ing of Universiti Malaysia Sarawak. The team concentrated on interviews and administering questionnaires in election campaign centres in Kuching, Asajaya, Samarahan and Simunjan. The team also followed closely election speeches given during the rallies organized by various political parties and independent candidates.

2 In the past a longhouse headman (*tuai rumah*) was elected through discussions held on the *ruai* (a roofed balcony) of the longhouse. A ballot was cast by a simple show of hands. When the Brooke and the British colonized Sarawak, they created and appointed other political positions, namely regional chief and paramount chief (Jayum A. Jawan 1944: 46; Sutlive 1992: 8).

3 The exchange rate before the July 1997 economic crisis was US$1 = RM2.50. After the imposition of selective capital controls in September 1998, the rate was fixed at US$1 = RM3.80.

4 It is true that, in general, logging activities are legal, but sometimes the licensed logging companies do not stop working in their given area. They often go beyond the fixed boundary. As a result, 'They destroy cultivated regions, plough through *temuda* (fallow rice fields) and fruit gardens and bulldoze graveyards' (Manser 1996: 90).

5 The Internal Security Act (ISA) was first introduced in 1960, when the twelve-year emergency was lifted by the Malayan government. The Act empowers the police to hold up to sixty days anyone who acts in a manner considered prejudicial to the security of Malaysia. The ISA gives the authorities wide powers of preventive detention. However, the ISA is now being used to curb freedom of expression and restrain people from criticizing the government.

6 Globalization and transnational class relations

Some problems of conceptualization

Abdul Rahman Embong

Introduction

An edited volume by McNall *et al.*, published in 1991, two years after the collapse of the Berlin Wall, bears a provocative title, *Bringing Class Back In: Contemporary and Historical Perspectives*. Two observations by its editors are pertinent to our discussion of globalization and transnational class relations. First, class is one of the most widely used and thoroughly contested concepts in the social sciences, with little agreement among scholars on its exact meaning or its explanatory power; and second, the study of class has been conspicuously absent in recent post-structuralist, post-Marxist and state-centred approaches emerging in historical and sociological scholarship (McNall *et al.* 1991). However, does this mean that class analysis has lost its analytical and heuristic power and usefulness? Or is it only going out of fashion, as something not currently intellectually trendy in the post-Cold-War era?

It will be argued that class analysis, while not trendy, is not losing its analytical power. Unlike changing cultural tastes and fashions, intellectual endeavours such as class analysis are something more lasting and profound, sharpened through the process of paradigm 'wars' and internal criticism necessary in advancing the frontiers of knowledge. Class analysis not only takes into account new approaches to sociological scholarship, but also sustains itself as a powerful, refined working tool in helping scholars understand the complexities of social and historical processes (McNall *et al.* 1991: vii). Although there have been some defects or inadequacies in the uses of class analysis, it remains relevant for understanding society provided that a fresh approach to the dynamics of class formation is adopted (Cox 1987). However, it should be stated from the outset that class analysis is not only complex and difficult, but its scope is also not exhaustive when analysing various levels of social structure. Class analysis does not replace other levels of analysis, including ethnicity, religion and gender. It should be seen as complementary to other analytical frameworks in examining various levels of social structure.

One problem in class analysis is that its focus has understandably been confined to classes within national societies, neglecting the transnational dimensions of class relations. These studies are often premised on the assumption that class formations are conditioned by the history, politics and culture of their respective societies. Such confines are in many ways justified because of the important roles classes, especially the emergent middle classes, play within national societies and the significance of class perspectives from the national viewpoint. This does not mean that such studies do not acknowledge the presence of representatives of the international bourgeoisie, international professionals and even international workers in their respective societies. The recognition of the international dimensions of class was already made over a century ago by the pioneers of class analysis. Marx and Engels, for example, did talk of the international dimensions of class. They highlighted the tendency of capital to nestle everywhere; representatives of the bourgeoisie went abroad to make investments, search for profit and form internal allies; and the proletariat also had their international counterpart, hence the slogan 'Workers of the world unite!' Several other writers also recognized the international dimensions of class.

As argued by a number of scholars (e.g. Cox 1987; Giddens 1997; Sklair 1991, 1997; Overbeek 2001), today, in the era of globalization, studies of class have to take into account transnational class relations. Just as capital, production, labour and culture have become globalized, classes too are increasingly becoming transnational. Globalization is a new phase in the development especially of finance capital, facilitated by the advancements in information and communication technology. In the contemporary era, there is a strong movement towards the integration of financial markets, with financiers, fund managers and finance consultants, alongside powerful industrialists, playing a critical role. At the same time, the media and advertising industry, owned and controlled by powerful business tycoons, have also become global, shaping opinions across the globe, influencing attitudes and lifestyles of various classes. This new situation throws a formidable challenge to social scientists everywhere not merely to study class relations nationally or regionally, but, more importantly, to study them transnationally. As noted by Giddens (1997: 64), with the processes of globalization becoming among the most important social changes today, sociological analysis that confines itself to single societies is becoming increasingly archaic.

While studying globalization and transnational class relations presents many theoretical and methodological problems, the core argument in this chapter is that production relations and the global system are dynamic concepts for starting the analysis of transnational class relations. To develop the argument, I will attempt to address the problematics of conceptualizing transnational class relations in the context of capturing globalization by focusing on three interrelated issues: (a) globalization and the reconfiguration of class relations; (b) emerging global class structure and the dominant class; and (c) subordinate groups *vis-à-vis* the dominant class. In the course of the discussion as well as in the conclusion, I will attempt to show in what way the various actors involved in the globalization process are at the same time forces for 'capturing globalization'. The pioneering works on transnational class relations by two eminent social scientists – Robert W. Cox (1987, 1996, 1997) and Leslie Sklair (1991, 1997) – form the starting point of my analysis. Cautioning that one should be careful not to overwork the concepts in our theoretical arsenal, this chapter raises several questions in the conceptualization of transnational class relations and offers some new propositions. Let us now address these issues in turn.

Globalization and the reconfiguration of class relations

Although globalization itself is a contested concept, this chapter does not take issue with it since it is the subject of earlier chapters. However, for the purposes of this chapter, globalization is defined as the compression of time and space aspects of social relations. It involves the acceleration of time and the reduction of spatial constraints, both of which have distinct consequences for all layers of society (Mittelman 1996a: 3; 1997: 14; Robertson 1992; Waters 1995).

The most powerful globalizing force that has reconfigured class relations is the transnational corporation (TNC), the emergence and expansion of which has unleashed the processes of deterritorialization of capital. Although capital had already become international especially since the nineteenth century, it was stamped with the characteristics of a 'national home' and nation-states to a certain extent could exercise some control over it. One could talk of British capital or US capital then. Since the 1970s, with the advent of a new phase of capitalism, characterized by the concentration of finance capital and the might of TNCs, it is difficult to assign a 'nationality' to such capital, except the country in which the TNCs are domiciled.

Successful TNCs do not see themselves as belonging to any country, but rather as separate non-national entities (Drucker 1997).

TNCs are involved in various activities on a worldwide scale, such as FDI, production, trade and financial transactions. According to some calculations, the amount of capital and assets of large TNCs has increased sharply over the last two decades. Several TNCs have annual incomes far bigger than the GNPs of many developing countries. For example, the total sales in 1992 of General Motors (amounting to almost US$140 billion), or of Exxon (amounting to almost US$120 billion), were much bigger than the GNPs of the oil-rich states of Saudi Arabia, or Indonesia, or even Norway in the same year.[1] At the same time, the development of information technology, namely computers and multimedia, facilitates the movements of finance capital, especially virtual money, at will with just a click of the 'mouse' (Singh 1999; Drucker 1997). According to estimates, more than US$1.5 trillion are transacted daily in the world's currency markets, and of this only 5 per cent are used in real production, whilst the rest are in the hands of fund managers for speculative purposes. These TNCs, integrated with the global system in a variety of ways, are run by managers and executives at different levels and from various countries. With the penetration of TNCs into various parts of the world, they have become more conspicuous and significant, exerting influence upon members of the domestic classes in the various countries in which they operate. These developments clearly demonstrate that globalization has reconfigured class relations transnationally.

Emerging global class structure and the dominant class

Given that globalization has reconfigured class relations, a major challenge in analysing transnational class relations is to map the classes that have emerged or are emerging transnationally. The global social structure is one of structured inequalities, consisting of dominant and subordinate groups, causing both conflicts and compromises between them. But what is the nature of this emerging global class structure? Who constitutes the dominant groups and the subordinate groups, and have they developed class consciousness?

To answer these questions, it is useful to do a mapping of transnational class relations so that we know the contours of the classes. However, constructing a class map is problematic not only for national classes, but also more so when analysing transnational class relations. Who are the members of the class that remains at the core of the global system? Is it the capitalist class or some other classes? In answering these questions, the difficulties revolve not only around determining the appropriate terminology and the components of such a class, but also around its characteristics, boundaries, consciousness, etc. Such difficulties can be seen in the attempts made by several scholars, namely Cox (1987, 1996), who uses the term 'transnational managerial class', and Sklair (1991, 1997), who refers to the 'transnational capitalist class'.

The first problem to highlight here revolves around the question of the constituent components of this class. The Coxian usage of the term 'transnational managerial class' implies a group of managers operating transnationally, who exercise control over the corporations. In this usage, ownership does not appear critical. In Cox's formulation, the dominant social groups comprise (a) TNC managerial cadres, i.e. those who control the big corporations operating on a world scale; (b) those who control big nation-based enterprises and industrial groups; and (c) locally based petty capitalists. Of the three that make up the dominant groups, the first, i.e. those controlling big corporations operating on a world scale, is the most important.

In Sklair's formulation, the term 'capitalist' is used as opposed to 'managerial'; thus he coins the term the 'transnational capitalist class'. However, to Sklair, the transnational capitalist class is not made up of capitalists in the traditional Marxist sense, defined in terms of the ownership of the means of production. As he puts it, 'direct ownership or control of the means of production is no longer the exclusive criterion for serving the interests of capital, particularly not the global interests of capital' (Sklair 1991: 62). He lists four social groups making up the transnational capitalist class, namely (a) TNC executives, i.e. the leading executives of the world biggest TNCs, supported by their local affiliates operating in various parts of the world; (b) globalizing bureaucrats performing governance functions for the global capitalist system at the local, national, interstate and eventually global levels where individual states are not directly involved; (c) capitalist-inspired politicians and professionals who perform a variety of personal and technical services for the maintenance of the global system; and (d) consumerist elites (merchants and media) who play important roles promoting global capitalism.

My reservation concerning Cox's and Sklair's approaches is their tendency to overwork their analytical tools, in particular their core concepts. Whatever the terminology, the main difficulty with the core concepts used by both scholars is that the constituent components of the dominant groups are too broad and amorphous. For example, the Coxian transnational managerial class includes not only the managerial cadres of TNCs and their families, but also public officials in the national and international agencies involved with economic management, as well as experts and specialists involved with the maintenance of the world economy in which the multinationals thrive and are supported by them. Among these experts and specialists are management consultants, business educators, organizational psychologists, electronic operators who assemble the information base for business decisions and lawyers who put together international business deals (Cox 1987: 359–360). What should be pointed out is that the ability of these various fractions to wield power and influence on the TNCs and the multifaceted arena in which the TNCs operate differs. Thus, lumping them into the same class as though they are homogeneous masks the heterogeneity of the groups and their differential standing in the hierarchy of power.

The concept becomes more unwieldy when Cox also includes in the transnational managerial class two other categories – national capitalists and petty capitalists. National capitalists by definition only operate on a national scale within nation-states, although the members may have an international dimension and their activities may increasingly become global in scope, being spurred by the processes of the internationalization of production, as argued by Cox. But they do not make much impact upon world order since they do not possess global clout. So, too, with petty capitalists, who are small capitalists operating on a more local scale. They are highly vulnerable to demand contraction in the domestic market and to high interest rates, leading to lower profits and even bankruptcies. They have little impact upon the global economy. Hence, it would appear odd to include both national and petty capitalists in the same category with TNC cadres as members of the transnational managerial class.

A similar critique can be advanced with regard to Sklair's formulation. His concept of the 'transnational capitalist class' is also overworked because too many fractions are included in the same category. His inclusion of the leading executives of the world biggest TNCs (including what he calls the 'consumerist elite' who control television networks and other media), supported by their local affiliates operating in various parts of the world in this class, is justified. Sklair is right in his assertion that the TNC cadres have a strong economic base, consisting of their corporate salaries and their often privileged access to shares and other financial privileges in the companies they work for either directly or as nominated board members. They thus wield immense power to the extent that they control parts of the global economy and their actions and decisions can have fundamental effects on the local communities in which their TNCs are located.

However, can other fractions – what Sklair calls 'globalizing bureaucrats, capitalist-inspired politicians and professionals' – be considered as constituent components of this core group or class? As he himself explains, globalizing bureaucrats are officials performing governance functions for the global capitalist system at the local, national, inter-state and eventually global levels where individual states are not directly involved. They either deal with or actually work in local urban and regional growth coalitions fuelled by foreign investments, in national bureaucracies responsible for external economic relations, or in international organizations such as the World Bank, IMF, Organization for Economic Cooperation and Development (OECD), WTO, regional development banks and some agencies of the United Nations. Capitalist-inspired politicians and professionals are a diverse group who perform a variety of personal and technical services in the global system. Sklair argues that while capitalist-inspired politicians respond to the interests of the corporations that provide employment and make profits locally, globalizing professionals have emerged as an important group in recent decades, owing to the expansion of business services industries, including think-tanks associated with neoliberal free trade and free enterprise agendas. Nevertheless, it should be pointed out that this latter group is too diverse and does not enjoy the strong economic base and power relations, as do the TNC executives. Thus, assigning members of this group the same class as the leading executives of the world's biggest TNCs is to ignore the most important criterion he himself uses, i.e. a strong economic base and the ability to wield power globally.

This does not mean, however, that the concepts are not helpful. On the contrary, they are novel concepts with strong analytical value. It would, nevertheless, be more useful and elegant to differentiate analytically the two concepts – the transnational capitalist class and the transnational managerial class – so that they are used to refer to distinct elements and that each concept becomes more focused. The first should refer basically to the TNC bosses and senior executives who are the main players in the global arena, making decisions and taking actions on behalf of their corporations; yet their actions can have an effect on the economies of the countries or regions in which they operate. Their economic base is not only their corporate salaries and various perks they receive from the TNCs, but also their shares in the various corporations they own or control, or in which they work or serve as board members. In terms of personalities, they may range from people like Bill Gates, Chief Executive Officer (CEO) and founder of Microsoft Corporation; Akio Morita, founder and head of Sony; Jun-Ichiro Miyazu, President of Nippon Telegraph and Telephone Corporation (NTT); George Soros of Quantum Fund; Stan Shin, Chairman and CEO of the Acer Group; and many others who feature in the *Fortune 500*. In fact, the world's 225 richest people – identified by *Forbes* magazine as 'the ultra-rich' – who have an estimated combined wealth of over US$1 trillion, equal to the annual incomes of 2.5 billion people, the poorest 47 per cent of the world's population (UNDP 1998: 30), can be said to constitute the core of the transnational capitalist class.

The transnational managerial class, on the other hand, should be used to designate the lower fractions within the dominant groups. This is more appropriate because in terms of their functions and power, they exist more in a 'supporting', 'advisory', or 'technical' capacity with regard to the global system – in short, they are 'managers' rather than 'controllers'. In countries where the TNCs have their locally based firms, those who constitute the top management may consist of local nationals. For example, of the sixteen member firms of the Malaysian American electronics industry in the mid-1990s, nine were under Malaysian managers including the managing director level (Mohd Nazri 1995: 148). However, unlike members of the transnational capitalist class, they do not decide on major policies or make system-wide decisions. Their economic base is weaker than the transnational capitalist class because it consists mainly of salaries and perks from their respective organizations. Although they may obtain earnings from shares, they are not substantial owners of the corporations in which they invest. This class is much larger in number than the transnational capitalist class and may consist of the capitalist-inspired politicians, bureaucrats, consultants, lawyers and other professionals who operate transnationally to service the TNCs in various ways. They are very influential, but cannot be put in the same league as members of the transnational capitalist class, as Cox's or even Sklair's formulation makes them out to be.

In sum, at the upper levels of the global social hierarchy are two major components of the dominant groups, the transnational capitalist class and the transnational managerial class, both of which operate to support the global capitalist system. The transnational managerial class is very important for the transnational capitalist class; it often serves the latter. However, the positions of these two classes are not fixed or static. Classes are dynamic entities that change their positions over time. For example, members of the transnational managerial class under certain conditions can ascend into the transnational capitalist class, while members of the latter too can fall into the transnational managerial class.

In defining the constituents of the transnational class relations, the main criterion is the scope and impact of their activities, i.e. whether they are involved in what is called 'transnational practices' (Sklair 1991). Classes that engage themselves in transnational practices can be said to have gone beyond their national boundaries and deserve to be considered as part of the transnational classes. On the other hand, classes that confine their activities mainly within the bounds of nation-states should be considered as national classes, not transnational ones. They may form part of the dominant groups domestically, but become subordinate groups when cast transnationally. On this basis, one should be guarded about including the national capitalists and the petty capitalists (Cox 1987) as part of the transnational managerial class. While globalizing bureaucrats, politicians and professionals who participate in transnational practices (Sklair 1991) may constitute the transnational managerial class, the national capitalists and petty capitalists are a different category. Their practices, in the main, are within national boundaries and though the former may have trading relations with some foreign partners, in the course of their evolution and expansion, they have to intensify and extend such relations before they can become part of the transnational managerial class or the transnational capitalist class.

The second problem is the question of class consciousness. A thorny issue even in national class studies, it becomes all the more complicated in transnational class analysis. Can one really talk of similar consciousness binding members of the dominant groups together? Or does the consciousness vary, with some fractions within the dominant groups wanting to maintain the capitalist system as it is while others may want to bring about reforms in global capitalism, giving it a more humane face as in Japan or in the Scandinavian countries? If one begins with a unitary conceptualization of the dominant groups, the conclusion will be that they exude a common class consciousness, thus downplaying their inherent differences. However, if one regards the dominant groups as heterogeneous, and can be conceptualized as two distinct groups or classes (the transnational capitalist class and the transnational managerial class), as suggested above, the inherent differences come to the fore.

Although both Cox and Sklair offer nuanced analyses concerning the differences within the dominant groups, they feel that they exist as a coherent class and possess a common class consciousness. Cox acknowledges that while TNC executives and their associates have interests that conflict with those of other class members, they neverthe-less share a common concern to maintain the system that enables the class to remain dominant. Cox draws attention to various institutions such as the OECD, IMF and World Bank that serve as foci for gener-ating policy consensus for the maintenance and defence of the world order. It is true that members of the dominant groups may be able to generate some consensus through these institutions, but issue-specific consensus and class consciousness may not mean the same thing.

The question of class consciousness becomes more contentious in Sklair's analysis. According to Sklair, the TNC executives and their associates are considered as one cohesive central class that makes system-wide decisions. The cohesiveness of this class is assumed to exist because many of its members occupy a variety of interlocking positions in a multiplicity of companies and in wide-ranging networks outside the corporate sector. They are said to have outward-oriented, global – rather than inward-oriented national – perspectives on a variety of issues; their members tend to be people from many coun-tries, who increasingly identify as 'citizens of the world', as well as by their places of birth; and they enjoy similar lifestyles and education, especially in business schools. They see their own interests and/or those of their nation as best served by an identification with the interest of the global capitalist system, in particular the interests of the countries of the capitalist core and the transnational corporations domiciled in them (Sklair 1991: 8). Sklair posits that members of the transnational capitalist class, embracing a culture ideology of global capitalist consumerism, do not identify with any foreign country in particular, or even necessarily with the First World, or the white world, or the Western world, but identify with the global capitalist system. They reconceptualize their several national interests in terms of the global system and take on the political project of reconceptual-izing the national interests of their co-nationals in terms of the global capitalist system (Sklair 1991: 117–118).

The problem with this conceptualization is that it assumes that in the era of globalization, nation-states as well as regional and other interests have been reduced to minor significance and that national classes are throwing in their lot with the transnational capitalist class. While many of the points raised by Sklair are true, to downplay or ignore the other interests is not tenable. Nationalism and regionalism are forces to be accounted for. It is true that the dominant groups share similar lifestyles, have a common interest in defending the global capitalist system, and their activities may have become transnational in scope, but have they also become transnational in their consciousness and put aside national or regional differences? In what way do they reconceptualize their several national interests in terms of the global system and take on the political project of reconceptualizing the national interests of their co-nationals in terms of the global capitalist system as argued by Sklair?

While the dominant groups may be united in their defence of the global capitalist system, it is doubtful if they become a cohesive central class. The fact that they are not as cohesive as they have been made out to be can be seen in the controversies surrounding IMF policies and decisions in handling the 1997–1998 financial crisis that began in Asia and spread to other regions. Also, there have been sharp differences, for example, between the TNCs originating from certain countries, such as France and those from the United States, as can be seen in the case of French oil corporations continuing to defy the US embargo on making contracts with Iran. At the same time, Japanese corporations insist that the Japanese government protect the domestic market by erecting protectionist walls against the intrusion of US interests. These events show that members of the dominant groups are not devoid of nation-state controls and influences. If we start from the premise that the dominant groups are heterogeneous, and their interests vary and often collide, then a common class consciousness cannot be assumed. They are committed to support and perpetuate the global capitalist system, but we cannot underplay the fact that they often operate from their own particular perspectives and interests in their actions. This fact often forms the basis for conflicts that intermittently occur among the different fractions within the dominant groups.

Subordinate groups *vis-à-vis* the dominant class

Who constitutes the subordinate groups in transnational class relations? Do they constitute coherent classes and a global force for change?

Globalization impacts on various countries in a number of ways. With the globalization of production, sections of the domestic classes become part and parcel of the global workforce in the service of the various TNCs. However, domestic classes consist of those involved in production in both the formal as well as the informal sectors. The key question concerns the criteria for analysing the relationship between the TNCs and the domestic classes. Should we only include those directly in the service of the TNCs, or those on the periphery, i.e. indirectly involved with the TNCs? To my mind, the emphasis should be on the former, but we cannot neglect the latter since they are also affected by globalization. For example, the 27 million electronic and other workers in the 800 export-processing zones (EPZs) worldwide (UNDP 1999) – in Malaysia, China, India, Brazil and other countries – share a common relationship since they are in the service of the various TNCs operating in these zones. But the common relationship does not apply only to workers and other employees in the EPZs. Others involved in service industries, such as banking, insurance, hotels, travel and tourism, that operate transnationally (e.g. those working as managers, executives, cashiers, tour operators, etc.) also constitute part of the global workforce. However, there are those on the periphery – hawkers, peasants, fishermen, the unemployed, casual labour and others – who remain outside the formal sector. They are peripheral to the TNCs, yet the latter impact their lives directly or indirectly. These forces, together with workers in the formal sector, constitute the majority of the world's population, who remain on the lower rungs of the global social hierarchy.[2]

It has been proposed that the subordinate groups consist of (a) the new middle stratum; (b) established (unionized) and non-established (non-unionized) workers; and (c) the peasantry and the marginals (Cox 1987, 1996). The new middle stratum, made up of technical, scientific and supervisory personnel in the most technologically advanced sectors of industry, has been regarded – depending on the researchers' theoretical perspectives – both as a 'new middle class' and as a 'new working class'. Researchers who label these personnel as the 'new middle class' see them as a buffer layer between owners of capital or those who control the accumulation process at the top and the mass of production workers below, while those who regard them as the 'new working class' see them as a force of change to resist globalization. Established workers, being unionized, enjoy a more secure position, while the fate of the non-established or non-unionized workers is rather uncertain. Together with them are large numbers of the peasantry and the marginals, i.e. those displaced from their land and who then flock to cities swelling the ranks of the unemployed and semi-employed. These latter people, found especially in peripheral countries, are excluded from the global economy (Cox 1987, 1996, 1997).

Those forces working with the TNCs and their affiliates objectively constitute the subordinate groups that are part and parcel of the global forces of production. Domestically, they may act as coherent classes, with the more advanced sections, having a certain

degree of class consciousness, but whether they constitute subordinate *transnational* classes is another matter. Unlike members of the
transnational capitalist class and the transnational managerial class
who operate transnationally and interact with one another, and who
are more mobile and transferable, the subordinate groups are mostly
workers operating within the bounds of the same country. This is not
to deny the fact that millions of workers have participated in
transnational migration in response to the reordering of global
production (Tabak 1996). There are massive transnational migrant
flows into Europe, North America, Southeast Asia and elsewhere. In
Malaysia, for example, before the July 1997 economic crisis, the
number of legal and illegal immigrants (including their families) was
estimated to be around 2 million, or about 10 per cent of the total
population. Nevertheless, both domestic and foreign workers, though
standing on the same side of production relations *vis-à-vis* the TNCs,
are not integrated with one another. Many do not share the same
language and lifestyles and they often do not identify with each other.
More often than not, the pull of ethnicity, gender, religion and geography – differences accentuated by globalization – is stronger than
the tug of class. All these limit their interaction and the possibility of
them being collectively organized to confront management and the
emergence of coherent subordinate transnational classes.

My point is that class membership is not sufficient to bring most
of these forces together as subordinate transnational classes and act
as coherent classes. They have to be organized and their consciousness raised. For a proportion of workers who are unionized and
whose organizations are affiliated to world trade union movements,
they may be quite outward looking and global in orientation, have
developed class consciousness and are in a better position to resist
the negative consequences of globalization. However, how they
respond to or resist the globalizing forces is contingent upon their
national and local experiences. For example, during the 1997–1998
economic crisis, while workers in South Korea and Thailand
unfolded militant struggles against retrenchment and other cost-
cutting measures by their managements, Malaysian workers, through
the tripartite employer–union–government machinery, negotiated for
reductions in pay and other benefits to save jobs.

For large masses of workers in many countries, unionization is still
an issue. Not all workers are unionized. This exclusion is especially
pronounced among workers in electronics, workers with lower skills
levels and more so among migrant workers – thus making them more
easily disposable and replaceable as a result of the 'restructuring' of

production by post-Fordism and during times of economic crisis. These precarious workers are an expanding category. The processes of exclusion of subordinate groups from transnational class organizations such as trade unions – thus affecting the growth and effectiveness of civil society – make them all the more vulnerable to the onslaught of capital and its representatives – the transnational capitalist class and the transnational managerial class.

Concluding remarks

In the preceding discussion, I have tried to show that class analysis in the post-Cold War era is still valid and that transnational class relations are an important topic for investigation today, especially in regard to globalization. Pioneers in this field, namely Cox and Sklair, have provided useful analytical tools to understand changing global social realities and the characteristics and roles of the transnational classes. The strength of their theories is not only that they can capture the complex global realities and explain them, but also they attempt to show a way out of the exclusionary processes of globalization. Nevertheless, studying transnational class relations is replete with theoretical and methodological problems, including the tendency to overwork one's concepts. We have to take note that while some members of the domestic upper class may have become transnational, we cannot assume the formation of transnational classes just because there are domestic classes that serve in global forces of production. It is important to bear in mind that just as globalization is a historical process, class formation too is a historical process, influenced by both national and international developments. Classes are simultaneously objective and subjective phenomena, both independent of their members' consciousness and expressed in conscious thought and practice (McNall *et al.* 1991: 3). I have argued that globalization has reconfigured class relations and transnational classes are in the process of formation, especially among the dominant groups and the more class-conscious and organized elements of the subordinate groups. But since the process is still in its early stages, the contours of the transnational classes have yet to crystallize fully.

In this analysis, I have shown that transnational class formation among subordinate groups is especially difficult. This is partly because, in the era of globalization, the lines among enemies, friends and allies are blurred, unlike the situation three or four decades ago when the targets of struggle were much clearer. At the same time, the exclusionary processes of globalization, especially the continuous post-Fordist restructuring, fragment large sections of the subordinate groups, more so among the unorganized, peripheral and migrant workers. Thus, resistance to globalization among subordinate groups often remains uncoordinated, diffuse and weak.

This analysis has also shown that globalization processes have produced contestations between different groups and classes domestically and transnationally. From the standpoint of capturing globalization, our analytical framework should take into account not only the subordinate groups, but also the various forces in the market and the state to identify the fault lines of globalization. That is why recognizing the inherent differences among the dominant groups and state actors, and to factor them in our multidimensional analysis of transnational class forces, is important.

Notes

1 Note the following facts which demonstrate the immense power of TNCs:

> Half of the hundred largest economic units in the world today are nations; the other half are transnational corporations ... The 600 largest transnationals account for more than one-fifth of the total industrial and agricultural production in the global economy. About seventy of these giant companies are responsible for half of total global sales ... The revenues of the largest 200 companies rose tenfold between the mid-1970s and the 1990s. Over the past twenty years, the transnational activities have become increasingly global: only three of the world's 315 largest companies in 1950 had manufacturing subsidiaries in more than twenty countries; some fifty do so today ... Eighty of the top 200 transnational corporations in the world are based in the United States, contributing just over half the total sales.
>
> (Giddens 1997: 295–296)

2 Global inequality is increasing, occurring in both the developed and developing countries. For example, while in 1960, 20 per cent of the world's people who live in the richest countries had thirty times the income of the poorest 20 per cent, by 1995 they had eighty-two times as much income. Today, while a small minority are extremely rich, about 1.3 billion people are in poverty, living on less than US$1 a day. One in four in developing countries (and one in eight in developed countries) is affected by human poverty and almost 1.3 billion people do not have access to clean water. Of 4.4 billion people who live in the developing countries, nearly 60 per cent still lack basic sanitation. Many in the poor countries such as in parts of Africa are objects of global poverty relief (UNDP 1998, 1999). This shows the existence of a huge gap between the rich and the powerful on the one hand and the poor and the weak on the other on a global scale.

7 Reconsidering cultural globalization
The English language in Malaysia

Sumit K. Mandal

Flows of culture appear decidedly one way in the constellation of processes that constitute contemporary globalization. The ubiquitous English language is a salient example. The language was once the preserve of a parochial people whom Defoe described in verse as 'a Mongrel half-bred Race ... With neither Name or Nation'. Today English dominates in the economy, diplomacy, the mass media, academia, education and popular culture across the globe. Cultural iconography from the United States with its own accent on English has made particularly visible inroads in many societies.

The language's global standing may not be as certain or as homogenizing as it seems. David Graddol's comprehensive study (1997) indicates that the dominance of English may be limited to particular transnational business, technological and communications networks of considerable power. Beyond these functional links, other languages remain viable and grow in significance within national or regional frameworks. Some even pose a challenge to English. The rise of distinctive variants rather than a unifying global standard of the language is another notable trend. English has acquired a culturally viable and hybrid local sensibility of its own in the former British colonies where the language has had a relatively long history. The localization of English as well as the ongoing viability of other languages point to the ascendancy of contradictory and contesting cultural flows. Flows of culture thus need not be one way.

This chapter grapples with the problems and possibilities offered by the expansion of English in Malaysia and thereby with cultural globalization on the whole. English has expanded vigorously in key areas of life following the state's embrace of globalization in the 1990s. In particular, it has made inroads in the corporate sector, technology, education and in the social life of major urban centres. The language's expansion is a salient indication of the impact of globalization in the country and brings with it disruptions in cultural identities that shed light on a principal question in the literature on globalization. Are externally driven forces transforming cultural identities after their own image? Or, do local actors play a role both in the promotion of global-izing trends as well as creating responses to them?

Neither the English language nor globalizing processes may be as totalizing as they seem, though both have caused cultural disruptions whose outcomes are not easily predictable. The term 'disruptions' as used here conveys a break in historically constituted cultural identities and not a state of chaos. In other words, the marked rise in English usage has posed challenges to the country's cultural identity and social values, however, with more than just adverse consequences.

The displacement of the national language *Bahasa Malaysia* (Malay) is the most obvious public manifestation of cultural disruptions. As such, this displacement becomes the focus of concern and criticism, frequently conveyed in little more than crudely ethnicized views of the complex issue (Ahmat 1994: 135–147). The language's rise is thus attributed to its promotion by some ethnic groups over others. Besides the ethnicization, this perspective limits itself to how much English has overtaken Malay rather than engaging the profoundly transformative economic, political and cultural processes that underlie its ascendancy. By reducing the problem to the competition between ethnic groups internally, this view turns critical attention away from realignments in the global political economy that have resulted in the active promotion of the English language. In sharp contrast, numerous scholars have developed critiques of the language's rise by paying attention to the global shifts in connection with the political and cultural complexities of particular societies. One scholar who has written extensively on the subject, Alastair Pennycook (1994), sees the self-conscious efforts at privileging English as a 'worldly' global commodity to be a manifesta-tion of contemporary neocolonialism.

This chapter argues that contesting processes are at work in the expansion of English and departs from the view that the language's rise has only threatened the country's cultural identity. On the one hand, the positivist, technocratic and economistic discourse of glob-alization sponsored by the state marginalizes long-standing elements of local culture. In this regard, the English language as an agent of globalization has affected cultural identity adversely. For example, the renewed focus on English in the late 1980s and 1990s reversed years of state planning in language issues that placed a priority on the national language. As such, English has gained a prominent place in the country's capital and public spaces on the whole.

On the other hand, English has been the source of much creative cultural production in Malaysia's ethnically and linguistically fragmented society. This is especially true since the national language has been ethnicized in keeping with the politics of the ruling elite and correspondingly bureaucratized because of its strong identification with officialdom (Mandal 1998). With a relatively lengthy educational, institutional and literary tradition in the country, the English language has been an important site for negotiating the colonial past and configuring a political community without respect to ethnic and cultural difference. Compelling artwork and ideas are advanced in this language that articulate a common local identity in creative ways and serve as a means by which Malaysians negotiate and resist the hegemony of cultural globalization.

Borrowing from Stuart Hall, this chapter rejects the view that globalization is merely a powerful set of uncontradictory processes leading to the homogenization of the world in culture, politics and the economy. Hall believes that more than any other time, globalization today has created conditions where 'the margins come into representation – in art, painting, in film, in music, in literature, in the modern arts everywhere, in politics, and in social life generally'. This movement is taking place, he notes, not 'to be placed by the regime of some other, imperializing eye but to reclaim some form of representation for themselves'. The margins come to represent themselves by 'recovering their own hidden histories' and retelling 'the story from the bottom up, instead of from the top down' (Hall 1998: 34–35). Given Hall's framework, the disruptions created by the ascendancy of English in Malaysia may serve as sites of contestation that empower those in the peripheries of cultural globalization.

The first of two parts in this chapter recovers the hidden history of English in postcolonial Malaysia by elucidating the prescient analysis of cultural resistance proposed three decades ago by Lloyd Fernando. This scholar of English literature, who was a professor at the University of Malaya until his retirement, provided a critique of the culturally homogenizing aspect of English in a number of his principal writings. The second part focuses on three contemporary Malaysian writers in the English language as examples of creative engagements with cultural globalization.

Framing cultural globalization with an eye to the margins

On 13 May 1969, interethnic violence broke out in the capital Kuala Lumpur and other parts of Malaysia precipitated by feuding political parties representing different ethnic groups. Little over seven months later, Fernando delivered his inaugural lecture titled 'English, Literature and Technology in South East Asia'. Although he addressed the episode of political violence only in passing, his lecture spoke volumes to the problems faced by the young nation with a multiethnic society bearing the heavy imprint of cultural, economic and political divisions of the British colonial past. Language was the site of some of the most fraught political and cultural conflicts of the time. A brief historical overview is necessary to contextualize much of the argument that follows.

The Malay language occupied a relatively marginal place in public life even some twelve years after independence. Its proclamation as the national language, as well as the creation of a state-run institution dedicated to its advancement, seemed to have done little to alter its position radically. Even though Malay had advanced in importance and scope, English still dominated much as it did under the British. The middle classes and elites of all ethnic groups were schooled in English, while the one university in the country not only operated fully in this language, but offered its first course in the Malay language only in 1970 (Fernando 1970: 4). The ascription by the British rulers in the past of a higher cultural value to English over Malay lingered on. While English was the language of social and economic opportunity to which a relatively small number had access, Malay, the language of the vast majority, provided fewer opportunities and was still held in some disregard.

The political violence of 1969 was the catalyst for great change. Fernando's lecture addressed Malaysia at the cusp of change as the state was about to embark on a long-term project of social and cultural engineering to redress the inequitable distribution of opportunities and wealth as well as cultural value. Soon after, the New Economic Policy was advanced as a long-term effort at eliminating poverty and the identification of economic function with particular ethnic groups. Malays were given particular attention, for they were largely relegated to the rural economy and relatively poor as a whole. At the same time, the state intensified its efforts to expand the reach and scope of the national language in order to forge a national culture and identity with Malay culture at its core. The National Culture Policy proceeded in 1971 and the constitution of a national culture was proposed in which the Malay language and traditions would form the core around which the languages and traditions of other ethnic groups would be incorporated.

Fernando presented a paper at the congress that formulated the National Cultural Policy and supported the move to regulate cultural affairs in the face of the decades of British intervention that led to the devaluation of local traditions. Reflecting his belief in the desirability and necessity of a unified national language, he lauded the proposal that literature written in the Malay language would be considered national literature while that in other languages would be considered sectional literatures (Fernando 1986: 138). In the subsequent decade, the Malay language advanced considerably as it replaced English as the medium of instruction in educational institutions.

It is within the context of the historical tension between English and Malay that Fernando's prescient analysis of the deep undercurrents in globalizing cultural tendencies stands out. He felt the promotion of Malay was a move of untold value, not only for restoring the dignity seized from it under the British, but also for fostering cultural solidarity in a multiethnic society. However, he was critical of the concurrent move to separate the teaching of English language from its literature, because it relegated the language to fulfilling the utilitarian role once filled by Malay (Fernando 1970: 6). In his mind, this pragmatic move would result in the comprehension of the English language without an understanding of its underlying values and cultural codes:

> [In] adopting English as a second language, as many South East Asian nations have done, we must necessarily give a place to the closest possible study of its literature because that is one of the surest ways of counteracting the intellectual hazards rooted in technological processes perfected in the West.
>
> (Fernando 1970: 25)

Not only was Fernando aware of the incipient ascendancy of the English language worldwide, he was also concerned about the transference of values associated with the processes that are collectively called 'globalization' today. He notes as follows about the need to be cognizant of the transformations wrought by the already rapid flow of information and images in the late 1960s by referring to the author of the term 'global village' that has since gained wide currency:

> The world is truly electric and simultaneous these days, and Marshal Macluhan's [*sic*] deterministic vision of us all being plugged into one vast electrical organism like domestic animals at a trough is far too close for us to laugh at it. In the pauses

between killing ourselves, indeed even while killing ourselves, we are truly hooked on the media.

(Fernando 1970: 15)

The subtle influences that Fernando feared would make Malaysians the slaves of technocracy were lost to state education planners. As such, the utilitarian approach to the teaching of the English language introduced in his time has taken root since, reflecting in equal measure the entrenchment of economistic readings of development. The economic liberalization programmes of the last decade have furthered the advance of economistic policies and values, thus resulting in the ascendancy of English for the very same utilitarian reasons of the past.

Fernando's work is a historical rereading from bottom up in more than one way and suggests strategic responses to globalization for those on the margins. In keeping with his advocacy of English literature, he strongly advanced the cultivation of complete bilingual fluency. On the one hand, bilingualism serves the pragmatic purposes of business, organizational, political and social communication across the globe. It also serves the important task of making available much needed reading material in Malay through translations of works in English. On the other hand, bilingual fluency affords translations that are sensitive to the particular cultural values of the language, whether in the act of translating writings or the more general process of understanding a variety of English-language cultural, political and economic spheres.

Bilingual fluency, Fernando believed, would lead to the dismissal of the fallacy submerged in English of its superiority to other languages in rendering the world in words. Fernando hoped for the following with respect to the acquisition of knowledge in English:

In other words, Malaysians will not be simple recipients in this process, struggling to reach 'levels' already achieved in the West, they will bring their own dynamics to bear, testing what they 'receive' against what is intrinsic in their own linguistic scheme.

(Fernando 1970: 28)

Fernando's hope of overcoming the ways in which English has been rendered culturally superior is not a flight of academic fancy. He is striking at the heart of the subservient behaviour instilled at the bottom end of relations of power, as in the self-hating figure of the colonized described by Fanon (1991). Independent Malaysia did not rid itself of this neocolonial mentality and globalization has brought it back with some vengeance, though differently.

One of the values encoded in the language of globalization is the inherent superiority of economistic thinking to politics and culture. And, in the hands of Southeast Asia's authoritarian political leaders – globalization's strongest local advocates – economistic measures have been applied to the near total exclusion of the deepening of political culture. In this regard, Fernando argues as follows in his critique of the continuous cultural fare offered by the mass media:

> It is imperative that while the economic battle in Asia is being waged, equally urgent care and attention must be devoted to raising the quality of the fare served up to us morning and night. Quality requires money. If industries are given pioneer status, why should not literature and the arts be given pioneer status too?
>
> (Fernando 1970: 24)

Fernando's views on language and culture are based on the conviction that human development in the broadest sense is at least as important as economic development, not only in terms of the restoration of dignity to the postcolonial self but for reasons more practical as well. For instance, he predicts the growing need for training in the humanities because globalizing trends had made it necessary 'to re-order in our consciousness myriads of facets of new knowledge, made available by the "information explosion" ' (Fernando 1970: 25).

As a scholar, Fernando has not been alone in embarking on the formidable task of reordering consciousness. Zawiah Yahya rereads the colonial English-language literary tradition in Malaysia in her 1994 book *Resisting Colonialist Discourse*. Although primarily an examination of the cultural politics of the English language, this book engages globalization in two significant ways. First, she shows that the English-language educational and literary tradition has been formative to the internalization by the colonized of self-abnegating discourses – a process with global ramifications. Second, by producing critical scholarship in English, hers is a notable example and reminder of working within this language towards intellectually and culturally liberating ends. Like Fernando, Zawiah shows that empowering scholarly work rests on a close understanding, rather than a simple rejectionism, of the colonizer's language.

Fernando locates some important ways in which globalizing cultural tendencies work and suggests strategies that for the most part rest on the affirmation of culture over solely economistic reasoning.

His ideas provide a critical framework and context for the following examination of Malaysian writing in English.

Three contemporary writers in English

Salleh Ben Joned, Rehman Rashid and Charlene Rajendran form the focus of the following discussion of Malaysian writing in the English language. This language has been critical to the country's literary and performance traditions as a whole. For instance, theatre in English thrives especially given the official openness to the language in the 1990s. Although confined to the middle classes and elites of Kuala Lumpur for the most part, theatre is unique for its imaginative enquiries into the country's multiethnic society. Veteran directors such as Krishen Jit explore the hybrid and pluralistic character of Malaysian society and thereby provide a sharp contrast to the ethnically divided political reality. This director alone has done much to create a tradition of theatre with a distinctly Malaysian idiom through productions in English, Malay, as well as those in multiple languages. Younger directors such as Jo Kukathas, Zahim Albakri and Huzir Sulaiman build on this tradition.

Within Malaysia's ethnically plural social and cultural environment, English has been an important site in which the search for a national self and political community has taken place. Historically, this search has occurred alongside the same efforts in the national language, though each linguistic sphere represented the aspirations and interests of particular social groups across the nation. Indeed, some of the first experiments in creating national forms of art and representation were self-consciously conducted in the English language. For example, Wang Gungwu published his collection of poems *Pulse* in 1950 with the deliberate intention of projecting images and subjects of a prototypical national identity (Lim 1994: 109–110).

This part does not provide a comprehensive overview of English writing in Malaysia but highlights three writers who span three generations as well as cross creative, linguistic and ethnic boundaries. Each in her or his own way engages local cultural politics and thereby gives form and breadth to local engagements with cultural globalization as well.

Salleh Ben Joned

Born in 1941, this writer is the oldest of the three. He has published a book of poems in Malay and English, typically excelling in both languages as few Malaysian writers can. His 1994 book of essays *As I Please*, however, is most pertinent in the present context.

Few have braved the ethnicized boundaries created by the politics of the 1970s like Salleh Ben Joned. His essays are critical of highly established personages in the literary and arts world whose authority as Malay writers and association with postindependent Malay 'nationalism' had once been undisputed. Often closely associated with official institutions, these Malay writers typically eschewed the English language on nationalistic grounds. However, the nationalism espoused was not inclusive and little else than chauvinism towards other ethnic groups. As a consequence, as an ethnic Malay writer with a more inclusive stance towards the country's cultural diversity, Salleh has often been regarded as an outsider if not a pariah.

Like Fernando, Salleh believes in bilingualism as a means of creating political community in the country:

> As far as English is concerned, its widespread use can, under the right conditions, be good for the nation because, like [Malay], English cuts across ethnic differences. Why regret the fact that our country has more than one *lingua franca*? Isn't it better for unity and integration?
>
> (Salleh 1994: 58)

Malay as the national language did not pose a problem in his mind, but its growing exclusive association with the Malay body after the 1970s is what has marred its progress. As such, he notes that English possesses the distinct advantage of not being identified with any ethnic group. Furthermore, he argues that within the Malaysian context the language can be a viable medium for local cultural expressions:

> A language belongs to those who speak it. It's as simple as that. Given this fact, and that language communicates experience and is capable of transcending the boundaries of the culture of its origin – given all this, then the English we speak in Malaysia today belongs to us. It's our English; along with [Malay] it expresses our 'soul', with all its contradictions and confusions, as much as our social and material needs.
>
> (Salleh 1994: 65)

Salleh's opinions on English and bilingualism are not based on instrumental or pragmatic reasoning alone. He holds strongly to the view that English is more than just a useful tool but an historical and essential part of creativity in the country.

Salleh's essays go well beyond divisive ethnic boundaries to create a unique and independent critical voice on the country's cultural politics. Indeed, it may well be his continued cultivation of English as a channel of his creative expression that has distinguished him. Others eschewed the language of their colonial education and promoted Malay only, thus eliminating a formative influence in their lives. Salleh cultivated his English educational heritage and thereby continued to engage the colonial past critically and in sum developed a deep appreciation of both Malay and English.

Rehman Rashid

Where Salleh provides illuminations of cultural politics, the journalist Rehman Rashid crafts a contemporary portrait of Malaysia since its independence in his 1993 book *A Malaysian Journey*. The book is a first in Malaysian writing because it embarks on two unprecedented journeys. First, its intellectual journey is solidly grounded in an all-embracing Malaysian perspective that does not privilege any one cultural group. Second, the travelogue takes the reader to every state in the country in an attempt to paint a portrait of the nation as a whole. The book thus provides a fresh means of envisioning the country's diversity of cultures, terrains and political communities.

It is instructive to ask why this important book was written in English. Part of the answer may lie in the author's own background, stories of which are woven into the narrative of the book. Born in 1955 to an English-speaking family and educated at the elite institution the Malay College, Rehman was moulded for the most part in the English language. English would 'give us the world', the author's father used to say in support of his insistence on the cultivation of the language (Rehman 1993: 81) At the same time, the choice of language may rest also on the openness of English, rather than Malay, to more inclusive perspectives, given the ethnicization of the latter after 1970. As such, English may have offered the author the freedom to explore anew the makings of the nation.

Besides a portrait of the country as whole, the book highlights the depth of the influence of the colonial era on cultural life. In an evocative description of his parents' different ethnic and religious backgrounds, Rehman notes how English was tied to early notions of political community:

A Malay, Muslim youth and an Indian, Christian girl: but their disparate ancestries had become intertwined in a common language, which was English, and united by what their generation was convinced had to be a common future, which was Malayan.

(Rehman 1993: 42)

In an earlier passage, the author learns that his schoolmaster grandfather had left diaries written in English that cited Shakespeare. Ismail Kassim Ali's diaries, however, expressed anti-colonial views in the same breath:

As they trample on the nationalities to reproduce London and Londoners in Asia, so they fear the hostility of ideas, of poetry, of religion – ghosts they cannot lay; ... they are tormented with fear that herein lurks a force that will sweep their system away.

(Rehman 1993: 36)

Rehman's reflections on English within his own family nicely raise the language's role in both the cultural subjugation of the colonized as well as the means by which anti-colonial politics was articulated. Rather than the rejection of this language, the excerpts affirm Fernando's insistence on mastery over the language and its literature as a means to empowerment.

Charlene Rajendran

Born in 1964, Charlene Rajendran published her first book of poems *Mangosteen Crumble* in 1999. A freelance theatre practitioner, teacher and actor, she has worked in a variety of Malay, English, and multilingual theatre productions. Her collection of poems is filled with words from a variety of linguistic influences – Tamil, Malay and Chinese. Aside from these, she writes poems in Malay and English as well as a mixture of the two.

Rajendran explores the cultural politics of English by examining her own identity. Where Salleh and Rehman engage the question of the national self directly, Rajendran does so by recovering her own history as a woman, the daughter of Sri Lankan Tamil immigrants and a member of a culturally diverse society. Like the other two writers, she is acutely aware of both the formative and problematic role of English. Indeed, her collection begins with 'Rasam Recipe', where in closing she casts doubt on her own admission of the primacy of English in her life:

And if I write in English
just because
the taste is mine,
it is my strongest condiment,
I've use it all my life
to spice and flavour piquancy,
does this mean I have
right?

does this mean I am
right?
                    (Rajendran 1999: 8)

English is inseparable from the Malay and Tamil cultural elements
referred to earlier in the poem, and all three are cast as essential
ingredients in the image evoked of the spicy broth called *rasam*. For
the poet, English is the 'strongest' of these different 'condiments'.
While the English language is problematized, the broth – representing
the cultural mix that constitutes her self – is privileged over language
in the same breath. Here Rajendran echoes Salleh's naturalization of
English for she admits the language as an integral part of her creative
self even as she recognizes it to be problematic.

Rajendran's embrace of English is liberating and empowering
rather than limiting. Where 'Rasam Recipe' began by problematizing
English, the first three stanzas of 'So *mush* of me' fully celebrate
the sounds of the admittedly colonial language – adjusted to the
Malaysian tongue – within the cultural mishmash that is her
identity:

So *mush* of me is English
my dreaded colonial heritage
from Enid Blyton to Beatrix Potter
My idylls lie distant in Yorkshire.

So *mush* of me lives in Anglo.
My dreaded white inheritance.
From Laura Ashley to Marks & Spencer
my istanas [palaces] all built in Windsor.

So, *mush* of me
misplaced.
Really I am Malaysian,
Ceylonese, Tamil,
Anglophile, All.

Mingled by history
not choice.
      (Rajendran 1999: 17)

Rajendran evokes a cultural identity through English, making the language resonate with the sounds and cultural references of her multiple and hybrid social worlds. She examines the national self by recovering the history of her own identity, thereby admitting the deep transformations set in motion by the English language since the colonial era. Her poems express a sense of self that may not be reflected in official rhetoric but resonates in the mixtures that do constitute Malaysian society, where languages are interchanged freely and English does not necessarily feel like an anomaly.

Three important themes occur in the works of Salleh Ben Joned, Rehman Rashid and Charlene Rajendran. First, the writers express their creativity in the English language with a self-awareness of the language's colonial origins and by making plain these problematic origins. In this manner, they recover a profound historical influence on the country that has been suppressed by the dictates of official nationalism. This subversive act frees them to exploit and even revel in the history and cultural resources offered by English in Malaysia. Second, they further the subversion by articulating the country's political community in terms of its multiethnic if not hybrid character. They present a world where languages and ethnic groups are not necessarily pitted against each other. Far from English eclipsing Malay, these languages as well as others are juxtaposed deftly to evoke the multilingual reality of Malaysian society. The country thus portrayed contrasts sharply with the communal party politics of its ruling elites. Third, the writers' engagements with Malaysian society and history in the first two themes create viable and grounded cultural, social and political spaces for engaging cultural globalization.

Conclusion

> To speak means to be in a position to use a certain syntax, to grasp the morphology of this or that language, but it means above all to assume a culture, to support the weight of a civilization.
>
>   (Fanon 1991: 17–18)

Speaking a language is not neutral activity, as Fanon observes pithily. In the discourse of globalization, English is claimed to be the most efficient and sensible language of trade and communication as the world's political economy becomes truly global in its reach. The language's rise in this regard heralds cultural and political transformations that discipline societies to adhere to a utilitarian and commercial regime of global proportions. English is the disciplining language of the transnational movement of capital, normalizing in its wake the universality of economistic values. Globalization thus is grounded in an ideology that transforms the variety of cultural identities in the world after its own image (Cox 1996: 23).

Proponents of English as the language of globalization include political, business and academic leaders in both the industrialized and industrializing countries. All of them speak the same language, its morphology and syntax is English, but its norms and substance denote transnational capital. Nevertheless, globalizers actively promote English as a purely functional and even neutral language that is synonymous with economic growth, technological advancement and modernity as a whole. Reflecting the influence of this idea, Malaysia's political leadership actively promotes English, quite innocent, it appears, to the deeper implications of the language's expansion in the country. The minister of education thus notes with little reflection: 'It is important for Malaysians to have a good command of English, particularly if we want to be an important global player' (Sprague 1999).

The language's presumed utility and superiority is at times stretched to speculative lengths. For instance, the noted economist Paul Krugman observes about the Asian economic crisis that began in 1997: 'The common denominator of the countries that have done best in this age of dashed expectations is that they are the countries where English is spoken' (quoted in Sprague 1999). Krugman does suggest that English proficiency may be linked to particular ideological leanings as would Pennycook, but this more plausible explanation is not further developed. All in all, his statement merely reinforces the belief that economic growth and efficiency is synonymous with English usage.

Like Fanon, Fernando has argued that language embodies culturally and historically specific perspectives and values. Critical of the global dominance of English, Fernando has observed persuasively that the spread of the language for purely pragmatic purposes brings with it serious hazards. He warns of the adverse consequences of assimilating the technocratic values and cultural constructions embodied by English as the language of globalization. Nevertheless, Fernando offers possibilities of resistance in the same language. Instead of rejecting the language, he advocates learning its literature to appreciate its civilizational breadth and thereby to develop a critical self-awareness in the language. This is a sure way he notes to counteract 'the intellectual hazards rooted in technological processes perfected in the West' and for Malaysians not to be simple recipients of Western notions of development.

The three writers discussed here exemplify the cultural resistance theorized by Fernando. Academics, arts practitioners and other social actors in Malaysia have foregrounded a lively hybrid cultural identity in which English has been localized and effectively made a lingua franca alongside Malay. In this regard, English is no longer the preserve of England, whether in terms of usage, scope, and perhaps more importantly, cultural authority (Graddol 1997: 3). In Malaysia, as in other former British colonies, postcolonial nationals have appropriated the language. Not only does English thus solidify local political community, it also serves as one way for Malaysia's cultural expressions to find a space in the world, or put in Hall's terms, for the margins to come into representation.

Contesting processes are at work in the case of English in particular and cultural globalization in general. On the one hand, globalizing ideologies and processes actively support and encourage the expansion of functional networks that expedite the one-way flow of cultural globalization. These networks evaluate and measure culture against pragmatic concerns such as economic efficiency. Importantly, they lay the foundations of an economistic and technocratic culture. In other words, the advance of economic globalization is inseparable from the cultural. On the other hand, social actors redefine the very terms of the economy by asserting the political and cultural in much the same way observed by Yoshikazu Sakamoto in his work on the formation of a global civil society (Sakamoto 1997: 218). Writers, artists, performers and other creative people provide alternative cultural frameworks that challenge globalization.

As seen in this chapter, creative cultural responses and resistance to globalization – capturing globalization – are articulated by recovering and retelling stories. The English language serves as a venue for renewed explorations of Malaysia's history, society and cultural identity, and is far from being an agent of cultural globalization alone. Social actors assert the cultural and political over the purely economic through these explorations. They demand of the proponents of globalization a more complex and pluralistic view of the economy, politics and culture. They speak a different language.

8 Capturing globalization
Prospects and projects

Norani Othman and
Clive S. Kessler

The common intellectual project informing the present book was centred upon four key questions. Framed and refined at the outset, these questions and the stance of the present writers towards them soon underwent far-reaching revaluation, made necessary by the events of 1997. At mid-year much of the world was mesmerized by the transfer of power and the return of Hong Kong to mother China, and looked in those dramatic events for some signs of the new importance of the Asian region as a whole in world society and the global economy. Meanwhile, scarce-noticed events were beginning to unfold to the southwest that would soon compel an urgent reassessment of the entire framework within which political leaders, investors and their economic advisers, and scholars – as well as everyday social actors – experienced and understood the ground on which they stood, the cosmos which they inhabited. Beginning with a 'run' on the Thai baht, not simply an 'Asian economic crisis' but, emanating from its Asian epicentre, a crisis of the entire world economy announced itself. If the post-Cold War world economy had been thought to stand on rock-solid foundations, this was an earthquake, perhaps the 'Big One'.

Far from requiring an abandoning of the four original questions, however, the events unleashed by the widening crisis only highlighted their significance and appropriateness; they dictated not a rejection of those questions but a new intensity and depth in our approach to them. The widening crisis highlighted both the inherent instability of the new worldwide economic order which highly mobile capital was in the process of creating and also its destabilizing social and political effects, most notably in the transitional societies which had recently engaged with those globalizing processes and proved so hospitable to their insistent partisans and publicists. By demonstrating both the inherent precariousness, even fallibility, of the economic globalization agenda and the costly human risks entailed by its often mindless pursuit or naïve acceptance, the 1997 economic crisis – and its continuing aftermath – showed that the results delivered by the globalization agenda and its sponsors were neither natural nor unproblematic. Rather, being neither necessary nor necessarily beneficial but contingent and humanly problematic, that agenda and the entire 'neoliberal' socio-economic rationale underpinning it needed to be subjected to close scrutiny and intense interrogation.

Neoliberal publicists may well be right when they insist that there are genuine and general social benefits which embracing such an agenda may deliver. But, even if attainable, these benefits are not immanent, unproblematically available, ready to be automatically delivered without any great human involvement, even travail, by those processes. Instead, if they are there to be had, they will only be identified and extracted as a result of careful intellectual analysis and discrimination, subtly directed human engagement, and informed political choice and intervention: in short, through the intelligent exercise of human judgement, capacities and agency.

Capturing, or captured by, globalization?

The chain of events unleashed by the 1997 economic crisis soon proved this point. But while they demonstrated in principle the necessity of human judgement and agency, they did not themselves indicate how, and where, these capacities might be exercised. This was the question which those events and their immediate implications posed for us. Our task as scholars was that of seeking to identify theoretically, even if in a preliminary or indicative way, just where and how human capacities and agency might actually be asserted within the very process of engaging with the logic, agenda and forces of ever-advancing globalization.

Hence the idea, and our leitmotiv, of 'capturing' globalization, the key recognition around which our various separate analyses revolve. Advancing globalization processes, especially if we passively submit to them as irresistible, may all too easily incorporate, subsume and in that sense 'capture' the people and societies drawn into their field of power. But, provided human agency and the human priorities of those people and societies are asserted from the outset within the process of engagement, there may indeed be genuine benefits for them to 'capture' from globalization. The key question accordingly is: who or what is to be captured – the people and their societies, for and by globalization and its sponsors, or the human benefits, by and also for those people and societies?

In other words, our theme provides two strategies for studying globalization. One approach is to seek to *capture an understanding of globalization* as a phenomenon – that is, to find out what it means in many societies currently caught up in it – and thereby to establish what kinds of social change are entailed by the whole gamut of processes labelled 'globalization'. This approach seeks to examine the nature and scale, the characteristics and effects, of globalization processes in their diverse economic, political, social and cultural contexts. Meanwhile, a second yet no less important avenue of enquiry must try to *capture concrete processes* of globalization. The aim of this line of enquiry is not merely to seek insight into the signif- icant underlying dynamics of the various processes subsumed under globalization, but also to devise effective means of capturing a measure of control over them.

The relationship between processes of globalization and the continuing economic growth and political stability of the societies engaging with globalization processes is of immediate political and human relevance. The financial crisis of the late 1990s and the ensuing economic downturn experienced by the nations of East and Southeast Asia have impressed upon many regional observers how crucial it is for states and societies at least to maintain some level of autonomy from the globalization initiatives urged upon their govern- ments; and beyond that, if possible, to assert a degree of policy control over their circumstances and consequences. While globaliza- tion processes may overall be irresistible, engagement with them, it is hoped, may be negotiable. If so, states have a role to play in framing these terms of engagement. If engagement with globalization processes is to be mediated, states need to devise policies rather than simply submit to the supposedly inevitable.

Yet the prospect of these states becoming merely 'captives' of the consequences of the globalization policies that they have implemented is altogether real. Recent experiences suggest that what actualizes and amplifies these potential risks is the intellectual and political abdication which follows from complacency: from complaisant acceptance by those with national policy-framing responsibilities of the often self-interested assurances of neoliberal theorists and experts that what the globalization agenda delivers is natural, irresistible and unproblematically beneficial. This strange alchemy by which some- thing can be both substantively neutral and positive at the same time has all too often been neither explained by the purveyors nor questioned by the avid consumers of the world's most widely prescribed economic medicine.

When developing countries liberalized and integrated their economies into the global economy, some of them were initially able to achieve rapid economic growth and market expansion. But that achievement was not without its costs and problems, some of which were revealed only later in that moment of crisis. In this context, to 'capture globalization' in the sense of asserting a degree of policy control over the terms of engagement can be seen to require rethinking the ideological bases of the neoliberal economic policies that uphold the virtue of financial globalization. Further reflection is now timely whether there exists any inherent and necessary 'logic' to globalization forces and to the process of state engagement with them. As economic globalization accelerates, political leaders must now consider whether nation-states have real choices anymore. What are the best choices? Is there only an enforced choice among a menu of options which all involve great risk and uncertainty? If so, how might one choose among them? Do any of them realistically offer, within the graspable future and not just as 'pie in the economic sky', the prospect of benefits that might warrant exposure to such risk?

This, for example, was the situation facing the Malaysian government when it began considering adopting a policy of capital controls in September 1998. Yet these were also the concerns lying behind our four orienting questions when we originally framed them: when the 1997 crisis still lurked unsuspected over the economic horizon, out of range of ordinary political vision; and when political leaders who were soon to 'go global' with their anguished denunciations of globalization and of the devious machinations of its sponsors, would hear no evil said, nor questions asked, about their policies of open embrace of global forces in a so-called borderless world.

A framework and six analyses

The primary yield of our effort to 'capture globalization' consists of an orienting framework and six case studies. This account of the project must conclude with a retrospective assessment of the match, or possible mismatch, between the framework and the analyses, between the questions posed and the case studies through which answers to them were sought.

The framework offered by James Mittelman provides the space and impetus for flexible, sceptical and undoctrinaire analysis. It rejects totalization. It refuses to see globalization as a unified phenomenon, a homogeneous bundle of processes, or an irresistible juggernaut. It suggests that, to be understood, the various developments subsumed by the term 'globalization' need to be disaggregated. Analytical disaggregation may in fact make the practical task of grappling with globalization, and seeking to capture whatever benefits it may have to offer, more feasible and amenable, less dispiriting and intimidating. In particular, he invites us to consider whether there may be any mutual tensions and dissonances, incompatibilities, or even contradictions, among the various dimensions and components into which 'globalization' may be disaggregated.

Not least among them, of course, must be the tensions between the forces of economic globalization, pushed by real human beings but which have lately assumed a breakneck and runaway impetus of their own, and the experiences of people worldwide who are subject to the diverse impact of those forces – between, in short, socioeconomic processes and human agency; between the unbounded transformative potential of those processes and the limits, especially the moral parameters, of human ontology. If these tensions exist, they are not merely technical, manifested in impersonal processes, but also human. But where, then, and how, are people to assert human concerns, and through human agency to inject their culturally informed moral content, into the new lifeworlds delivered to them by globalization?

Put this way, this is undeniably a political question. But we are left to ponder where the best, most strategic, sites for such human intervention are. Clearly, the nation-state is not dead and has an indispensable role (one which pro-globalization ideologues tacitly acknowledge in the force of their assault, both practical and ideological, against the state and its capacities for resistance). More than just 'bringing the state back in', we need to counter the sedulously cultivated myth of its contemporary powerlessness (Weiss 1998). But the experience of globalization also requires us to consider other sites and venues of potential human reassertion as well: from substate and transnational arenas to the countervailing spaces of civil society which stand alongside state structures but apart from them.

Of the six studies, it is, unsurprisingly, the two detailed analyses by the economists Rajah Rasiah and Ishak Shari which strongly suggest the juggernaut power of the forces of globalization and their unequal effects: the huge benefits which they permit to accrue to the powerful globalizers; the growing overall gap, absolute or relative, between the beneficiaries and the objects, the captors and captives, of globalization. Private capital flows, Rajah Rasiah suggests, and the industrialization which they promote serve capital and the large metropolitan investors directing it best, delivering far more to them than to the economies and societies in which they find hospitality and a temporary home.

Not only international but also domestic inequalities are accentuated, at least in the short run (and who will live to see and enjoy the long run?), by the impact of economic globalization, Ishak Shari argues. If economic development is not just an end in itself but a means to human development generally (and the partisans of globalization too often simply, without argument or evidence, assert the latter, while being content with the realization merely of the former), then the fruits of globalization are few and somewhat bitter. Economic development is stimulated and occurs, but in a form which accentuates existing inequalities, creates new ones and which lowers general standards of social equity: not just by increasing income differentials, one might argue, but by reducing overall levels of human welfare benefits ('the social wage') which governments deliver – feel obliged and are willing and able to deliver – to the populace as a whole. Such reductions entail effects not merely in material standards of living; they reduce the moral content and human meaning of citizenship itself.

Yet the economic development driven by globalization is not without its local as well as overseas or international beneficiaries. There are also at the domestic level, if on a smaller scale, winners and losers, captors and captives. Ishak Shari's analysis highlights the growing economic gap, and by implication the declining levels of social equity, that result from this kind of development: the kind long ago characterized by the great Dutch sociologist of Southeast Asia W.F. Wertheim (1964) as the policy of 'building and betting on the strong' – and letting the weak, those left behind or too naïve or poorly placed to seize the new opportunities, look after themselves. Declining levels of popular support for and satisfaction in government performance, especially the performance of governments committed to development through headlong globalization, are not at all surprising in this context.

Abdul Rahman Embong notes the same phenomenon, the same tendency. Globalization, he indicates, delivers most of its benefits to its metropolitan backers and their own domestic supporters, political constituency and audience. But some benefits do nonetheless accrue in the target society, or at least at certain social levels within it. A new middle class emerges and is consolidated that would not otherwise have come into being; but its growth is based not upon any sharing in the main fruits of globalization, but rather from the quite modest leftovers from the globalizers' sumptuous banquets.

We might borrow here a term from Gramsci and his followers among Indian historians to characterize this new middle class, concentrated for example in the vast new housing estates and suburbs of Kuala Lumpur and Jakarta: they are the 'subaltern' beneficiaries of globalization, its 'subaltern captors'. The members of this new aspiring middle class have much to lose, materially and socially, if their assumptions of uninterrupted and rapid economic development are disappointed; but many of them are also impelled by the advances they have already made into middle-class life and attitudes to be at least a little sceptical of bland government assurances that all remains well in the post-1997 world. Evidence of such doubts and ambivalence has been accumulating throughout Southeast Asia in recent times. The potential for social and political discontent among this growing class is considerable: in bad times, it may well find overt expression; but in good times, it may remain contained by a general contentment with the fruits of 'subaltern embourgeoisement'. As subalterns, they are in a sense both captors and captives.

To suggest such open-ended possibilities is to begin to 'detotalize' and 'disaggregate' globalization and its impacts: to acknowledge a potential divergence between what globalization delivers, and is intended to deliver, economically and its human effects and reception. In less self-conscious times, some might have spoken of the dialectical tensions between the economic and social dimensions of globalization, between its material effects and its effects at the level of human experience and consciousness. Similar considerations are raised by Sabihah Osman's analysis of the response of the indigenous peoples of Sarawak, on the island of Borneo, to encroaching globalization, especially as manifested in the clear felling of tropical rainforests by a rapacious timber industry. On the one hand, they have been subjected to these processes and thereby separated from their ancestral lands and the way of life and cultural identity which access to those lands supported; on the other hand, they have also learned during their painful experience of that process of separation that their predicament is not unique, but part of a worldwide process whose travails others also suffer. They have learned, too, to respond, to act politically, to seek to counter those developments by drawing upon insights, knowledge, strategies and political understandings which, no less than the logging industry, have come to them as part of their experience of globalization.

But the contest is a far from equal one. It pits the indigenous peoples of Sarawak not only against the timber industry and barons but also against the state itself. If the state is seen by many as a potential bulwark against the excesses of rampant globalization, it can also be their facilitator. In Sarawak, the role of the state has not been insufficient but excessive. Both the nation-state, at the federal level, and the state of Sarawak, at the regional or provincial level, have thrown their weight behind the logging industry and joined forces with it. In their political struggle, the indigenous Sarawak peoples have been confronted by, and have had to confront, a powerful industry, domestically based but of global reach, and also the combined power of the nation-state centralized in Kuala Lumpur and the Sarawak state government: both of which are committed to forms of elite interethnic coalition making whose logic marginalizes the once definitive peoples and cultures of western Borneo as merely small and backward ethnic minorities. The play of globalizing forces and their human impact here is complex and far from univocal.

More of this kind of complex, even dialectical, interplay between the various forces, effects, dimensions and experiences of globalization is evidenced in the analyses of Clive Kessler and Sumit Mandal. The former recognizes within the dominant dimension of globalization an impetus impatiently seeking to make the world one on its own terms. But at the same time, this same dynamic – quite unsought, even despite the intentions of the main enthusiasts and beneficiaries of economic globalization – gives rise and provides actuality to a hitherto only dreamed-of kind of universal human interdependence: one which, unprecedentedly, may provide a secure social as well as moral foundation for the effective affirmation of human dignity and human rights worldwide. The emergence of this new moral universalism – a new arrival in the history of the human moral imagination – is not only catalysed by the processes and experiences of globalization; it also furnishes a powerful intellectual, political and moral critique of, and the grounds for resisting, the excesses of globalization itself.

Sumit Mandal's account of language and identity in contemporary Malaysia finds similarly paradoxical effects produced by the advancing linguistic hegemony of English which the forces of globalization have demanded and delivered. There is a real and growing economic value to English, one which provides a marked 'competitive advantage' to those societies where command of English is substantial and widespread. But this favouring of English, by international economic logic as well as through explicit developmentalist government policies, comes at a cost: to the social status and economic value of major national languages indigenous to the region before the latest onslaught of globalizing processes.

Yet this is not an entirely negative development. Through English and its growing centrality as a lingua franca of international modernity, issues of identity and cultural inclusion are being creatively resolved as well as just posed. New forms of social and political identity – reaching across class, regional and internal ethnic lines of division as well as across international boundaries throughout the Southeast Asia region – are being shaped within English-language discourse. New kinds of subjectivities and political consciousness are being promoted which are far broader than, and which therefore can challenge and defy, narrower forms of identity: those presumed by sectional ethnic affiliations, the national identities promoted by official state-sponsored nationalisms and those marketed by essentially 'Americanizing' agendas of globalization.

If at the economic and social levels, the story written by globalization is largely polarizing – between the hegemonic and the subaltern, between captors and captives – the cultural situation delivered by economic globalization is far more mixed, multivocal and pluralistic. There is here perhaps a lesson, and the grounds for some hope, for all who would capture something of value from whatever advancing globalization may have in store for humankind.

Four questions in search of some answers

Four key questions, like the four horsemen of an impending apocalypse, stand behind the chapters contained in this book, driving the analyses offered by their various authors. While those questions have oriented the analyses offered, they in turn, it is hoped, also throw some revealing light back upon those questions and help frame some answers to them. Not just answers to the questions but some answers about the nature of the questions themselves: not just whether they are appropriate and interesting questions but whether the four questions, separately, admit of simple, unequivocal answers; whether, together, they add up or not to some coherent and inclusive account of contemporary globalization experiences; whether they might support some persuasive and overarching explanatory 'narrative'.

Do globalization processes serve any ends outside themselves?

The first of them poses the question whether the globalization agenda rests upon any distinctive moral values or ethical foundation, whether it delivers and institutionalizes any coherent normative order of its own. The partisans and enthusiasts of advancing globalization treat it, and speak of it, almost as a force of nature: one that is irresistible and, being beyond judgement, neutral, but also as a force whose moral core and actual impact are nonetheless positive, good and equally good for all. But this, our analyses suggest, is not true. So we must address the question whether contemporary globalization processes are simply opportunistic and largely incoherent or whether they do promote a coherent ensemble of values, a distinctive set of interests or coherent agenda – and, if so, whose?

It is hard to identify any simple 'villain' or beneficiary behind advancing globalization processes, in all their contending diversity; perhaps only a committed conspiracy theorist seriously hopes, or imagines, that such a bogeyman can really be found pulling all the strings and overseeing a single coordinated plan from somewhere offstage. Not even those who railed against George Soros, it seems, really believed that he was the coordinating evil genius. They simply singled him out as a convenient image or 'signifier'. He was chosen to symbolize, and more than that actually to personify, what those who had come to regret their earlier enthusiasm for untrammelled globalization later found themselves up against. Feeling personally betrayed and ill-used, they sought to give expression to, and even find relief for, their personal anguish by portraying the newly acknowledged adversary in quite personal terms. If a single bogeyman did not exist, he had to be invented, using a borrowed George Soros 'identikit'.

But to recognize that there is no single bogeyman masterminding globalization, and no single set of interests or values that can be unambiguously identified as the obvious beneficiary of contemporary globalization processes in all their bewildering diversity, is not to assert that globalization delivers no identifiable moral 'package', just a grab-bag of diverse and mutually indifferent or unrelated values. There is a moral code that moves and a moral vision that lies immanent within the gamut of most globalization processes, a social imagination that it delivers and promotes.

Strangely, it is the very same social imagination that Emile Durkheim, notably in his critique of Spencer but in fact throughout his entire life's work, sought to contest as the nineteenth century was ending and the twentieth beginning: the view that the modern social world consists of individuals and nothing more; that these individuals are formed and in turn form their preferences and choices not as complexly interconnected social beings but as separate, virtually self-sufficient atomized entities; that the preferences which they value and the choices which they pursue are essentially material and quantifiable in nature; that society is nothing more than the sum of its individual members and that individualism is not itself a complex socially constructed moral order.

In other words, the social theory which Durkheim elaborated was an empirically grounded utopia, or at least the moral basis for one, that stood opposed to the counterfactual and quite ideological dystopia, the quite asocial social vision, of modern neoclassical economics with its imagined world of atomized, isolated, satisfaction-seeking, strategizing individuals. Closer to our own time, Margaret Thatcher articulated anew Spencer's vision when she famously, and perhaps self-contradictorily, asserted that there is no such thing as society, just a whole lot of individuals seeking to make their own way in it.

Without having any single mastermind or serving any one tight knot of interests, contemporary globalization agendas promote a certain social and moral imagination: that of the direct lineal descendant of the social world imagined by the neoclassical economics which a century ago Durkheim opposed – late twentieth- and early twenty-first-century neoliberalism. It is an imagination which, after recognizing that as bodied and therefore separate beings we can and must act as individuals, wrongly infers from that fact that we can only act as, and are therefore nothing more than, separate individuals; and which, when applied to situations being transformed by the impact of modern economic changes, threatens at great human and social cost to actualize and thereby make true that false inference. This transformation takes hold through an essentially simple but cumulatively complex feedback process described below: a 'recursive' dynamic (Giddens 1987: especially 11 and 44) whereby mundane ideas and even powerful doctrines *about* social reality, through their acceptance into human consciousness and the actions it informs, are fed back *into* and thus become a constitutive part of evolving socio-cultural practice; a similar notion is also fundamental to Geertz's notion (1973: 3–30) of the 'cultural analysis' of the ideas which people draw from and subsequently feed back into the flow of social life.

Human content: grasping the best, making the most, of globalization?

If globalization, while embodying a certain ideologically driven social imagination, does not necessarily promote any specific set of interests or promote any detailed and unambiguous social agenda, we are faced at least in principle with an attractive option, an encouraging possibility. If the agenda which globalization may deliver has not been set in advance, then it is to some degree open ended. Within that space, we may then have some possibility of inflecting, shaping, or even of putting a little of our own preferred content into the package which globalization processes will deliver to us. At least, perhaps, we may have some small chance of avoiding the worst that globalization might otherwise impose.

A hopeful possibility; but how are we to avail ourselves of it? There was a time, just at the threshold of modernity, when Marx and Engels had not yet glimpsed in their Communist Manifesto the world of constant accumulation and accelerating transformation on a global scale which contemporary globalization theory still seeks to grasp; and when the neoclassical economics later challenged by Durkheim had not yet succeeded in imposing its own foreshortened moral vision as the master discourse of late modernity. It was a time when leading social theorists looked forward to the production of a new social order. They dreamed (a dream that was later adopted within orthodox Marxism) of reordering the everyday social world through the devising and application of policy, general and impersonal: a reordering based upon replacing the government of people with the administration of things. In those times, still under the shadow of personal absolutism, advanced thinkers envisioned human freedom and opportunity as being encouraged, and permitted to thrive, by substituting technocratic impersonalism for the vagaries and arbitrariness of royal and noble prerogative.

The successors of those early social and policy scientists have by now realized their dream, that of Durkheim's predecessors the Saint-Simonians, and have made of it a nightmare which we now inhabit. They have delivered us into the 'cold, steel-like housing' or 'iron cage' which Max Weber dimly perceived as the tragic trajectory of modernity itself. We have had enough, and more, of impersonality and instrumental rationality, of the supremacy of technical calculations over substantive moral considerations. We yearn for a return of human concerns, a restoration of human beings in their integrity, at the centre of the social planning and processes shaping our lives around us. We now want to dream, and also realize, a new dream that will counter that of the brave yet naïve Saint-Simonians.

We want to reorder human lives, to reconfigure our now disfigured human existence and to reaffirm the moral meaning of human beings: by overturning the administration of people as if they and we were just things. Whether the Saint-Simonian dream can now be reversed is unclear; but that is the challenge with which the human dilemmas of contemporary globalization now confront us. More than a challenge, the task of 'capturing globalization', or just seeking to do so, provides us with a timely and even historic opportunity to put that possibility, and ourselves, to the test. To make the most and get the best out of globalization, or just to avoid the worst, we will have to find ways and identify the strategic points to inject our own preferred human content into globalization processes; to contest and socialize the asocial neoliberal vision which underpins today's dominant forms of globalization; and to place a human imprint upon and thereby inflect in humanly sensitive ways the powerful forces which all too often embody a debasing preference for the administration of things over the vital integrity of human life.

Market logic: subject to cultural inflection and political supervision?

What globalization processes deliver, and what their sponsors and partisans demand, is the worldwide spread, the universalization, of market logic. This outcome entails the setting aside or stripping apart of the myriad different local cultural logics that had previously informed economic life, as an embedded part of social life generally, in the various areas newly brought within the reach and grasp of global economic forces. It requires (in Karl Polanyi's terms) the 'disembedding' or liberation of economic processes from their wider social milieu, their autonomous construction as 'an economy' operating on its own strategizing and 'satisfaction'-maximizing logic.

Globalization and the consequent incorporation or subsumption of hitherto culturally distinctive societies within the one emerging global order corrodes the pre-existing cultural logic of those societies, beginning in the realm of economic activity but fast ramifying out to all other domains of social life. The question is: after stripping back those pre-existing cultural values and logics, does advancing globalization substitute in their place any distinctive cultural values and logic of its own? Or does it simply strip away the old cultural encasement from human action, leaving universal human nature based upon its inherent individualistic motivations and psychology to stand free, 'value free' as it were?

The market model, the logic of the incessantly strategizing individual or *homo economicus*, is praised and promoted by its champions as corresponding with essential human nature as, without ideological illusions or preconceptions, 'it really is'. That, they say, is why it works and why other economic ethics and philosophies don't: it alone is consistent with essential human nature, while all others by denying it entail human unfreedom and market distortion. As they go about promoting its worldwide institutionalization, the partisans of this model see and laud it as impersonal, impartial and universal: as embodying general human nature and intentionality, not any specific or parochial cultural paradigm.

But the fact that this model of the choice-making price-driven economic actor is inevitably abstract and impersonal does not entail that it is morally impartial, free of all cultural bias, or neutral in its social effects. On the contrary, the model carries its own ethical bias, moral logic and social imagination: that of Milton Friedman's and Margaret Thatcher's fiercely competitive individualism; the view that individualism is natural, self-sufficient and free standing rather than socially constructed; that societies are no more than the sum of their individual members; and that social ethics and institutions are nothing more than the negotiated products of consciously contracting market actors. That this moral model is formally abstract and impersonal does not mean, however, that it is impartial or neutral in its effects. On the contrary, when applied to unequal situations, formally impartial value systems are unequal in their impact and consequences. The individual-istic model serves best the interests of those who are able to act powerfully as individuals. It systematically favours, in the main, indi-viduals who are already advantageously placed, while its formal impartiality disguises the fact that this is how it operates and these are its inequality-intensifying effects.

More, the initially false description of the human situation which the market model offers becomes self-validating. Not just a descrip-tion, it is also a model, one which constrains reality to conform and align itself with the model's own characterization of human ontology. It not only says that humans are solely and exclusively, primarily and overwhelmingly, or else essentially self-seeking strategizers; it also approves and endorses as self-evident that this is how they are and must be. Rightly so, there is no alternative, the theory insists. Individuals are induced to act in that way which the theory endorses. Those who do are rewarded with success and power, those who do not are not; those who conform deserve to be rewarded and are, those who do not conform deserve nothing and get just about that. As individuals, their moral sensibilities and social behaviour are increasingly brought into line with this model; the model itself increasingly becomes an accurate description of and guide to reality.

Those who do not align themselves with it become not only fewer in number but, in consequence, increasingly atypical and even deviant. In the end the theory proves and justifies itself; human beings enlist themselves to it and thereby transform economy and society, finally making real the market model's dream of a society of competitive individualists. This is its culture.

The question whether markets can be made culturally sensitive, whether they may be institutionalized on different cultural bases and according to alternative cultural logics, and whether on that basis they can be directed and regulated, restrained and governed by extra-market political means, is not a simple one. Were the market simply as 'value free' and neutral as its more simplistic champions declare, it might be possible to inject into real markets varying cultural contents or biases, consistent with local needs and histories. But these are the views of partisan advocates, not undoctrinaire analysts. The more realistic sponsors of globalization, however – the insightful and less illusioned advocates of the universal institutionalization of market principles – know that their model is not culture free. They recognize that it has its own cultural contents and biases; and that it therefore needs to be defended not in 'naturalistic' terms through debates over 'human nature' but in ideological terms, on the grounds of human 'freedom'. Nineteenth-century political liberalism must be shrunk into late twentieth-century economic 'neoliberalism', and individual human freedom of choice and movement must somehow be made coterminous with, and to find their apotheosis in, the freedom of capital and the rights of those who oversee its global movements.

What this recognition suggests is that if the advance of market principles and culture is to be resisted, modulated, or mediated in any way, that objective cannot be attained simply in the realm of economics. A successful reply can only be both cultural and political: one that makes explicit the moral bias and then challenges the cultural content and social effects of the market model of the human actor. That task is inescapably political. It requires not just an intellectual critique of market ideology; it also requires that its narrowed social imagination be challenged by juxtaposition with an alternative, more multivalent and inclusive social imagination. That challenge cannot be made simply through intellectual juxtaposition. Market morality and social theory can only be effectively confronted by an alternative that has been posed not just in intellectual polemics but, at least in initial prototype, in some socially institutionalized form. Whether or not it amounts to a form of 'counter-hegemony', this alternative must at least counter the hegemony of the market model in some socially institutionalized, politically constructed form. In other words, there are no easy answers, only hard work: 'the strong and slow boring of hard boards', in Weber's (1948: 128) powerful words.

Globalization: a 'package-deal'?

Peter Berger (Berger *et al.* 1973: especially 98) once spoke of modernity as a 'package-deal'. But then modernity itself, or so its postmodernist critics allege, is a totalizing project and would have to imagine and offer itself on a 'package' basis. But what, in this era of advancing anti-modernist scepticism, about globalization: is it too a 'package-deal'? Mittelman (this volume) is surely right when he suggests that globalization is not 'a single unified process but a set of interactions'. But, in turn, do those various different interactions and their manifestations in the various domains where they occur display any overall coherence, or are they mutually indifferent, perhaps even contradictory?

There is no a priori reason to assume they must all add up to a consistent package, be mutually reinforcing, or even mutually compatible. On the contrary, if we concede any plausibility to Immanuel Wallerstein's view (1999: *passim*) that the historical system of world capitalism is entering a period of transformatory crisis, then we should expect that system and its globalizing impetus to display certain dissonances or elements of incoherence and tension, even entropy. This scenario, as Wallerstein outlines it, is decidedly scary; but it is one in which the possibilities for human agency, and for human intervention to prove effective, may increase significantly. That is, the prospects for the kind of political challenge to globalization processes, or at least to the moral vision and the kinds of cultural content which they deliver, that was adumbrated in the previous section may be, in the midst of darkening times, brighter than they might now seem.

That is, not only need we not expect globalization to display any unified features or a single face; there may be genuine grounds for hope in the fact that it does not. These political implications aside, the analytical implications of the same fact are also noteworthy. They suggest that we need, while recognizing the single historical moment of their present occurrence and its common imprints, to disentangle the various strands of contemporary globalization processes, to differentiate among their forms and vectors, and disaggregate their effects. If, contrary to their enthusiasts, globalization processes, as we have suggested, do not together add up to any simple, obvious, natural, irresistible good, then perhaps they don't add up, and we don't need them to add up, to anything at all. They may just amount to a very mixed, contingent, jumbled and mutable 'package': one whose various contents may change in intensity and even character, independently of one another, over time. If this is so, then – the small freedom of political space it may afford and the grounds for modest political optimism which it may justify aside – this 'open verdict' on the common and coherent nature of globalization's manifestations is, appropriately for our times, a very postmodern one: that globalization too displays no common explanatory logic or simple master narrative.

If this 'open verdict' is warranted, then we are released from the grip of dispiriting determinisms and politically disabling teleologies. If all is not foreordained and foreclosed, to the extent that things are open ended and variable, they are also, at least in principle, negotiable: provided those who wish to have some say in how they encounter and engage with the various forces of globalization can astutely recognize not just their negotiability but actually where and how they can be engaged on other than purely their own terms. The retreat of the OECD-sponsored Multilateral Agreement on Investment (MAI) in 1998 – after NGO-driven public disquiet prompted a number of prospective signatory countries to have second thoughts about the great surrender of sovereignty entailed – and the chaotic outcome of the WTO meeting in Seattle in late 1999, when street demonstrations frustrated a high-level intergovernmental meeting and action on its international agenda, may, for better or worse, be instructive here. The central issue is to understand, intellectually and also practically, the politics of this engagement. It is a question of pursuing and enacting an appropriate analysis: of understanding possibilities and limitations; of identifying in which domains, and at which critical junctures, globalization processes may be subject to political contestation, to countervailing human intervention, to responsive negotiability. Demonstrating the possibility of such intervention may not only make globalization, and those who promote it, in some measure accountable. It will also be a reassertion of human capacity and moral choice, a rescue of the human moral imagination from the grip of 'dismal' economism, a reaffirmation of the moral nature of human beings.

There is a strange, even pleasant, irony here. At the height of the Cold War, one of the free-market champions' standard political critiques of the Moscow alternative was that socialism, or Stalinism, by its adherence to its core tenet that 'economics drives all else', was materialistic and soulless. Only liberal capitalism could appreciate – could find space for, and scope for the expression of – complex human values and realities. Now, as impatient globalization processes accelerate in the immediate post-Cold War era, that same economistic heresy reigns as the dominant rhetoric of neoliberal 'public ideology'. Not old liberalism, but those who would resist its brash new offspring are those who now uphold, and seek to redeem, the moral meaning of human beings and human existence.

Bibliography

Adorno, T. (1974) *Minima Moralia: Reflections from Damaged Life*, trans. E.F.N. Jephcott, London: Verso/New Left Books.

Ahmat, Adam (1994) *Isu Bahasa dan Pembentukan Bangsa*, Kuala Lumpur: Dewan Bahasa dan Pustaka.

Akyuz, Y. and Gore, C. (1996) 'The Investment-Profit Nexus in East Asian Industrialization', *World Development* 24(3).

Alarcon-Gonzalez, D. (1995) 'Trade Liberalization and Income Distribution: Lessons for Mexico from East Asia', *Mimeo*.

Albrow, M. (1996) *The Modern Age*, Stanford, CA: Stanford University Press.

Amsden, O. (1989) *Asia's Next Giant*, New York: Oxford University Press.

Badriyah Hj. Salleh (1991) 'The Problems of Land Tenure System in Sarawak During the Brookes', Paper presented to the 12th IAHA Conference 23–28 June, Hong Kong.

Baran, P. (1973) 'Development of Underdevelopment', in C.K. Wilber (ed.) *Political Economy of Development and Underdevelopment*, New York: Random House.

Baumann, Z. (1998) *Globalization: The Human Consequences*, Cambridge: Polity Press.

Berger, P., Berger, B. and Kellner, H. (1973) *The Homeless Mind: Modernization and Consciousness*. New York: Random House.

Best, M. (1999) 'The New Competitive Advantage', *Mimeo*.

Borneo Bulletin 19 July 1987.

Borrego, J., Alvarez, A.B. and Jomo, K.S. (eds) (1996) *Capital, the State and Late Industrialization: Comparative Perspectives on the Pacific Rim*, Boulder, CO: Westview.

Case, W. (1993) 'Malaysia: Semi-Democratic Paradigm', *Asian Studies Review* 17(1–7): 75–82.

—— (1997) 'Malaysia: Still the Semi-Democratic Paradigm', *Asian Studies Review* 21(2–3): 79–90.

Chang, H.J. (1994) *Political Economy of Industrial Policy*, London: Macmillan.

Chomsky, N. (1998) 'Free Trade and Free Market: Pretense and Practice', in Fredric Jameson and Masao Miyoshi (eds) *The Cultures of Globalization*, Durham, NC: Duke University Press.

Chossudovsky, M. (1997) *The Globalisation of Poverty: Impacts of IMF and World Bank Reform*, Penang: Third World Network.

Chowdhury, A. and Islam, I. (1993) *The Newly Industrializing Economies of East Asia*, London: Routledge.

Cox, R. (1987) *Production, Power, and World Order: Social Forces in the Making of History*, New York: Columbia University Press.

—— (1996) 'A Perspective on Globalization', in James Mittelman (ed.) *Globalization: Critical Reflections*, Boulder, CO: Lynne Rienner.

—— (1997) 'Gramsci's Thought and the Question of Civil Society in the Late 20th Century', revised version of a paper presented to the Conference on Gramsci, Modernity, and the Twentieth Century, held in Cagliari, 15–18 April 1997.

Crouch, H. (1996) *Government and Society in Malaysia*, Ithaca, NY: Cornell University Press.

Department of Statistics Malaysia (Sarawak Branch) (1998) *Monthly Statistical Bulletin Sarawak*, Kuching (February).

Deyo, F. (1989) *Beneath the Miracle: Labor Subordination in East Asia*, Ithaca, NY: Cornell University Press.

Dicken, P. (1998) *Global Shift: Transforming the World Economy*, 3rd edn, New York: The Guilford Press.

Drucker, P.F. (1997) 'The Global Economy and the Nation-State', *Foreign Affairs* 76(5): 159–171.

Ellis, B. (1998) *First Abolish the Customer: 202 Arguments Against Economic Rationalism*, Ringwood, Victoria: Penguin Books.

ESCAP (1999) *Economic and Social Survey of Asia and the Pacific 1999*, New York: United Nations Organization.

Fadzilah Majid Cooke (1997) 'The Politics of "Sustainability" in Sarawak', *Journal of Contemporary Asia* 27(2): 217–241.

—— (1999) 'Forests, Protest Movements and The Struggle Over Meaning and Identity in Sarawak', *Akademika*, Bangi, University Kebangsaan Malaysia, 55 (July).

Falk, R.A. (1994) 'Democratizing, Internationalizing, and Globalizing', in Yoshikazu Sakamoto (ed.) *Global Transformation: Challenges to the State System*, Tokyo: United Nations University Press.

Fanon, F. (1991) *Black Skin, White Masks*, New York: Grove Weidenfeld.

Fernando, L. (1970) *English, Literature, and Technology in South East Asia*, Kuala Lumpur: University of Malaya.

—— (1986) *Cultures in Conflict: Essays on Literature & the English Language in South East Asia*, Singapore: Graham Brash.

France, A. (pseud., Jacques Anatole François Thibault) (1894/1924) *Le Lys Rouge* (*The Red Lily*), trans. Winifred Stephens, London: John Lane/Bodley Head.

Friedman, T.L. (1999) *The Lexus and the Olive Tree: Understanding Globalization*, New York: Farrar, Straus and Giroux.

142 Bibliography

Froebel, F., Heinrich, J. and Kreye, O. (1980) *The New International Division of Labour*, Cambridge: Cambridge University Press.

Galbraith, J.K. (1998) 'Wall Street Insanity Now Has a Perfect Cover' (Interview with B. Laurance and W. Keegan), *The Sunday Sun* (Kuala Lumpur), Business Focus Section, 12 July: 26.

Gaspar, C.M. (1997) 'Globalization and the Indigenous Peoples: Focus on Malaysia. The Philippines and Mexico', *Kasarinlan*, A Philippines Quarterly of Third World Studies, Manila: University of the Philippines.

Geertz, C. (1973) *The Interpretation of Cultures: Selected Essays*, New York: Basic Books.

—— (1998) The World in Pieces: Culture and Politics at the End of the Century, *Focaal: Tijdschrift voor Antropologie* 32: 91–117.

Gerschenkron, A. (1962) *Economic Backwardness in Historical Perspective*, Cambridge, MA: Belknap Press.

Giddens, A. (1987) 'What Do Sociologists Do?' and 'Nine Theses on the Future of Sociology', *Social Theory and Modern Sociology*, Cambridge: Polity Press, pp. 1–21 and 22–51.

—— (1990) *The Consequences of Modernity*, Cambridge: Polity Press.

—— (1991) *Modernity and Self-Identity: Self and Society in the Late Modern Age*, Cambridge: Polity Press.

—— (1997) *Sociology*, 3rd edn, Cambridge: Polity Press.

—— (1998) *The Third Way: The Renewal of Social Democracy*, Cambridge: Polity Press.

Gill, S. and Mittelman, J.H. (eds) (1997) *Innovation and Transformation in International Studies*, Cambridge: Cambridge University Press.

Gough, E.K. (1968) 'Anthropology and Imperialism' (also headed 'Anthropology: Child of Imperialism'), *Monthly Review* 19, xi(April): 12–27.

Graddol, D. (1997) *The Future of English?*, London: British Council.

Gray, J. (1993) *Beyond the New Right: Markets, Government and the Common Environment*, London: Routledge.

—— (1998) *False Dawn: The Delusions of Global Capitalism*, New York: The New Press.

Hall, S. (1998) 'The Local and the Global: Globalization and Ethnicity', in A.D. King (ed.) *Culture, Globalization and the World-System: Contemporary Conditions for the Representation of Identity*, Minneapolis: University of Minnesota Press.

Hamilton, C. (1983) 'Capitalist Industrialization in East Asia's Four Little Tigers', *Journal of Contemporary Asia* 13(1): 35–73.

Harakah 14 June 1999.

Hartcher, P. (2000) 'James Wolfensohn's Ultimate Challenge', *Australian Financial Review Magazine* April: 25–31.

Harvey, D. (1990) *The Condition of Postmodernity: An Enquiry into the Origins of Cultural Change*, Malden, MA: Blackwell.

Hasan Mat Nor (ed.) (1998) 'Warga Pribumi Menghadapi Cabaran Pembangunan', Jabatan Antropologi dan Sosiologi, Universiti Kebangsaan Malaysia, Occasional Paper No. 8.

Heilbroner, R. (1993) *21st Century Capitalism*, New York: W.W. Norton.

Held, D. (1991) 'Democracy, the Nation-state and the Global System', in D. Held (ed.) *Political Theory Today*, Cambridge: Polity Press.
—— (1995) *Democracy and the Global Order*, Cambridge: Polity Press.
Held, D., Goldblatt, D., McGrew, A. and Perraton, J. (1997) 'The Globalization of Economic Activity', *New Political Economy* 2(2): 257–277.
Held, D., McGrew, A., Goldblatt, D. and Perraton, J. (1999) *Global Transformations: Politics, Economics and Culture*, Stanford, CA: Stanford University Press.
Henderson, J. (1990) *Globalization of High Technology Production*, London: Routledge.
Higgott, R. (1999) 'Bank from the Brink? The Theory and Practice of Globalization at Century's End', Paper presented at 13th Asia-Pacific Roundtable, Kuala Lumpur.
Hirst, P. and Thompson, G. (1996) *Globalization in Question: The International Economy and the Possibilities of Governance*, Cambridge: Cambridge University Press.
Hoogvelt, A. (1997) *Globalization and the Postcolonial World: The New Political Economy of Development*, Baltimore, MD: Johns Hopkins University Press.
Huntington, S.P. (1996) *The Clash of Civilizations and the Remaking of World Order*, New York: Simon & Schuster.
Hurst, P. (1990) *Rainforest Politics, Ecological Destruction in Southeast Asia*, Kuala Lumpur: S.A. Majeed.
Hutton, W. (1995) *The State We're In*, London: Jonathan Cape.
Ignatieff, M. (1984) *The Needs of Strangers*, London: Chatto & Windus.
—— (1999) *The Warrior's Honor: Ethnic War and the Modern Conscience*, London: Vintage Books.
INSAN and authors (1992) *Logging Against the Natives of Sarawak*, Petaling Jaya: Institute of Social Analysis (INSAN).
Ishak Shari (1999a) 'Bumi Semua Manusia: Menangani Ketidaksetaraan Ekonomi dalam Arus Globalisasi', *Syarahan Perdana* (Inaugural Lecture), 15 September, Bangi: Universiti Kebangsaan Press.
—— (1999b) 'Economic Growth and Income Inequality in Malaysia 1971–1997', *Mimeo*.
—— (2000) 'Economic Growth and Income Inequality in Malaysia, 1971–95', *Journal of the Asia Pacific Economy* 5(1 & 2): 112–124.
Ishak Shari and Ragayah Mat. Zain (1997) 'Economic Growth and Equity in Malaysia: Performance and Prospects', in Ahmad Mahdzan (ed.) *Southeast Asia on the Growth Path: Book of Readings*, Serdang: Universiti Pertanian Malaysia Press.
Jameson, F. and Masao, M. (eds) (1998) *The Cultures of Globalization*, Durham, NC: Duke University Press.
Jayum A Jawan (1994) *Iban Politics and Economic Development: Their Pattern and Change*, Bangi: Universiti Kebangsaan Malaysia.
Jomo K.S. (1986) *A Question of Class*, Kuala Lumpur: Oxford University Press.

—— (1996) *The Southeast Asian Misunderstood Miracle?*, Boulder, CO: Westview.

—— (1999) 'The Damn Dam Returns to Haunt Malaysia', in *Harakah*, Kuala Lumpur.

Jomo K.S. and Ishak Shari (1986) *Development Policies and Income Inequality in Peninsular Malaysia*, Kuala Lumpur: Institute for Advanced Studies, Universiti Malaya.

Kessler, C.S. (1978) *Islam and Politics in a Malay State: Kelantan 1838–1969*, Ithaca, NY: Cornell University Press.

—— (1985) 'The Cultural Management of Death: Individual Fate and its Social Transcendence', in M. Crouch and B. Hüppauf (eds) *Essays on Mortality*, Kensington Studies in the Humanities and Social Sciences, Faculty of Arts, University of New South Wales, pp. 135–152.

—— (1991) 'Negotiating Cultural Difference: On Seeking, Not Always Successfully, To Share the World with Others – or, In Defence of Embassy', *Asian Studies Review* 15, ii(November): 57–73.

Khondker, H.H. (1997) 'Globalization Theory: A Critical Appraisal', in H.M. Dahlan, Hamzah Jusoh and Hing Ai Yun (eds) *ASEAN in the Global System*, Bangi: Penerbit Universiti Kebangsaan Malaysia.

Khor, K.P.M. (1997) 'The Southeast Asian Financial Crisis', *Mimeo*.

King, A.D. (ed.) (1993) *Culture, Globalization and the World-System: Contemporary Conditions for the Representation of Identity*, Minneapolis: University of Minnesota Press.

King, V.T. (1990) 'Why Sarawak in Peripheral?', in Victor T. King and J.G. Parnwell (eds) *Margin and Minorities: The Peripherals Areas and Peoples of Malaysia*, Hull: Hull University Press.

Krongkaew, M. (1994) 'Income Distribution in East Asian Developing Countries: An Update', *Asian-Pacific Economic Literature* 8(2): 58–73.

Leigh, M.B. (1974) *The Rising Moon: Political Change in Sarawak*, Sydney: Sydney University Press.

Lim, S.G. (1994) *Writing South East/Asia in English: Against the Grain*, London: Skoob.

Loh, Kok Wah Francis (1998) 'Pluralism and Democracy in Malaysia: Political, Cultural and Social Challenges', Working paper at Seminar on Islam, Culture and Democracy, A Regional Roundtable, IKMAS, Kuala Lumpur and SIS Forum Malaysia, 17–18 August.

Long, T.E. (1991) 'Old Testament Universalism: Prophetic Seeds on Particularistic Soil', in R. Robertson and W.R. Garrett (eds) *Religion and Global Order*, New York: New Era Books/Paragon House, pp. 19–34.

Machiavelli, N. (1985) *The Prince*, trans. H.C. Mansfield, Chicago: University of Chicago Press.

Mahathir Mohamad (1999) 'Globalization: A Double-Edged Sword?', in *Mainichi Shimbun* 29 January.

Maiguashca, B. (1994) 'The Transnational Indigenous Movement in a Changing World Order', in Yoshikazu Sakamoto (ed) *Global Transformation: Challenges to the State System*, Tokyo: United Nations University Press.

Malaysia (1971) *Second Malaysia Plan 1971–1975*, Kuala Lumpur: Government Printers.

—— (1989) *Mid-Term Review of the Fifth Malaysia Plan 1986–1990*, Kuala Lumpur: Government Printers.

—— (1991) *The Second Outline Perspective Plan 1970–1990*, Kuala Lumpur: Government Printers.

—— (1994) *Mid-term Review of Sixth Malaysia Plan*, Kuala Lumpur: Government Printers.

—— (1999) *Mid-term Review of Seventh Malaysia Plan, 1996–2000*, Kuala Lumpur: Government Printers.

Mandal, S.K. (1998) 'Bahasa Inggeris dan Keperibadian Nasional', *Pemikir* 13: 59–86.

Manne, R. (1998) *The Way We Live Now: The Controversies of the Nineties*, Melbourne: Text Publishers.

Manser, B. (1996) *Voices from the Rainforest*, Petaling Jaya, Malaysia: Bruno Manser Foundation and INSAN.

Marx, K. (1960) *Capital: Volume One*, London: Pelican Books.

—— (1970a) *Capital: Volume Two*, London: Pelican Books.

—— (1970b) *Critique of Hegel's 'Philosophy of Right'*, ed. & intro. J. O'Malley, Cambridge: Cambridge University Press.

—— (1975) 'A Contribution to the Critique of Hegel's Philosophy of Right: Introduction' (*Einleitung*), in *Karl Marx: Early Writings*, intro. L. Coletti, trans. R. Livingstone and G. Benton, New York: Vintage Books, pp. 243–257.

McGee, T.G. (ed.) (1986) *Industrialization and Labour Force Processes: A Case Study of Peninsular Malaysia*, Canberra: Australian National University.

McGrew, A. (1992) 'A Global Society?', in S. Hall, D. Held and A. McGrew (eds) *Modernity and Its Future*, Cambridge: The Open University.

McNall, S.G., Levine, R.F. and Fantasia, R. (1991) *Bringing Class Back In: Contemporary and Historical Perspectives*, Boulder, CO: Westview.

Mehmet, O. (1986) *Development in Malaysia: Poverty, Wealth and Trusteeship*, London: Croom Helm.

Mittelman, J.H. (ed.) (1996a) *Globalization: Critical Reflections*, Boulder, CO: Lynne Rienner.

—— (1996b) 'Rethinking "the New Regionalism" in the Context of Globalization', *Global Governance: A Review of Multilateralism and International Organizations* May–August: 189–214.

—— (1997) *Globalization, Peace and Conflict*, Bangi: Universiti Kebangsaan Malaysia Press.

—— (1999) 'The Future of Globalization', Pok Rafeah Chair Public Lecture, Institut Kajian Malaysia dan Antarabangsa, Bangi: Universiti Kebangsaan Malaysia.

—— (2000) *The Globalization Syndrome: Transformation and Resistance*, Princeton, NJ: Princeton University Press.

Mohd Nazri Ismail (1995) *Transnational Corporations and Economic Development: A Study of the Malaysian Electronics Industry*, Kuala Lumpur: University of Malaya Press.

Nam, S.W. (1993) 'Korea's Financial Markets and Policies', *Mimeo*, Seoul: Korea Development Institute.

New Straits Times 8 July 1991.

Norani Othman (1999) 'Grounding Human Rights Arguments in Non-Western Culture: Shari'a and the Citizenship Rights of Women in a Modern Islamic State', in Joanne R. Bauer and Daniel A. Bell (eds) *The East Asian Challenge for Human Rights*, Cambridge: Cambridge University Press.

Ohmae, K. (1991) *The Borderless World: Power and Strategy in the Interlinked Economy*, New York: Harper Perennial.

—— (1995) *The End of the Nation State: The Rise of Regional Economies*, New York: Free Press.

Onchan, T. (1997) 'Income Distribution and Poverty in Thailand', in Ahmad Mahdzan (ed.) *Southeast Asia on the Growth Path: Book of Readings*, Serdang: Universiti Pertanian Malaysia Press.

Overbeek, H. (2001) 'Transnational Historical Mechanism: Theories of Transnational Class Formation and World Order', in R.P. Palan (ed.) *The New Global Political Economy: Theorizing and Approaches*, London: Routledge.

Panitch, L. (1996) 'Rethinking the Role of the State', in J. Mittleman (ed.) *Globalization: Critical Reflections*, Boulder: Lynne Rienner.

Pateman, C. (1989) *The Disorder of Women: Democracy, Feminism and Political Theory*, Cambridge: Polity Press.

Pennycook, A. (1994) *The Cultural Politics of English as an International Language*, London: Longman.

Phoa, J. (1996) 'The Dayaks and Orang Ulu of Sarawak', in C. Nicholas and Raajan Singh (eds) *Indigenous Peoples of Asia: Many Peoples, One Struggle*, Bangkok: Asia Indigenous People Pact.

Polanyi, K. (1957) *The Great Transformation: The Political and Economic Origins of Our Time*, Boston: Beacon Press.

Porritt, V. L. (1997) *British Colonial Rule in Sarawak 1946–1963*, Singapore: Oxford University Press.

Pusey, M.R. (1991) *Economic Rationalism in Canberra: A Nation-Building State Changes its Mind*, Cambridge: Cambridge University Press.

Rajendran, C. (1999) *Mangosteen Crumble: A Book of Poems*, Kuala Lumpur: Team East.

Rao, B. (1988) 'Income Distribution in East Asian Developing Countries', *Asian Pacific Economic Literature* 2(1): 26–45.

Rasiah, R. (1990) 'The Relocation of the Electronics, Textiles and Garment Industries in Southeast Asia', *Mimeo*.

—— (1994) 'Capitalist Industrialization in ASEAN', *Journal of Contemporary Asia* 24(3).

—— (1995a) *Foreign Capital and Industrialization in Malaysia*, London and New York: Macmillan and St Martin's Press.

—— (1995b) 'Labour and Industrialization in Malaysia', *Journal of Contemporary Asia* 25(1).

—— (1996) 'Industrialization and Income Distribution in Taiwan', *Mimeo*.

Rasiah, R. and Chua, T.C. (1998) 'Strength of Trade Unions in Southeast Asia', in R. Rasiah and V.H. Norbert (eds) *Workers on the Brink*, Singapore: Friedrich-Ebert Stiftung.

Rasiah, R. and Hofmann, V.N. (eds) (1996) *Liberalization and Labor*, Singapore: Friedrich Ebert Stiftung.

Rasiah, R. and Ishak Shari (1997) 'Malaysia's New Economic Policy in Retrospect', in H.M. Dahlan, Hamzah Jusoh, A.Y. Hing and J.H. Ong (eds) *ASEAN in the Global System*, Bangi: Universiti Kebangsaan Malaysia Press.

Rasiah, R., Jomo K.S. and Ishak Shari (1996) 'Globalization and Liberalization and Its Implication for Growth, Poverty and Inequality in East and Southeast Asia', in A. Wood (ed.) *Globalization, Liberalization and Its Implications for Growth, Poverty and Inequality*, Geneva: UNCTAD.

Rehman Rashid (1993) *A Malaysian Journey*, Kuala Lumpur: Rehman Rashid.

Ritchie, J. (1993) *A Political Saga: Sarawak 1981–1993*, Singapore: Summer Times.

Robertson, R. (1990) *Power and Economy in Suharto's Indonesia*, Manila: JCA Press.

—— (1992) *Globalization, Social Theory and Global Culture*, London: Sage.

Rodrick, D. (1994) 'Getting Interventions Right: How South Korea and Taiwan Grew Rich', NBER Working Paper No. 4964.

Rosenau, J.N. (1997) *Along the Domestic-Foreign Frontier: Exploring Governance in a Turbulent World*, Cambridge: Cambridge University Press.

Sakamoto, Y. (1994) 'A Perspective in Changing World Order: A Conceptual Prelude', in Yoshikazu Sakamoto (ed.) *Global Transformation: Challenges to the State System*, Tokyo: United Nations University Press.

—— (1997) 'Civil Society and Democratic World Order', in S. Gill and J.H. Mittelman (eds) *Innovation and Transformation*, Cambridge: Cambridge University Press.

Salleh Ben Joned (1994) *As I Please: Selected Writings 1975–1994*, London: Skoob.

Salleh Buang (1999) 'Bakun Dam "Tradegy" Revisited', *The Sun on Sunday* (Kuala Lumpur), 20 June.

Sanib Said (1985) *Malay Politics in Sarawak 1956–1966: The Search for Unity and Political Ascendancy*, Singapore: Oxford University Press.

Sassen, S. (1998) *Globalization and Its Discontents: Essays on the New Mobility of People and Money*, New York: The New Press.

Schneider, M. (1998) ' "Economic Rationalism": Economic Rationalists and Economists', *Quadrant* 42, x(October): 48–53.

Scott, A. (ed.) (1997) *The Limits of Globalization: Cases and Arguments*, London: Routledge.

Sennett, R. (1998) *The Corrosion of Character: The Personal Consequences of Work in the New Capitalism*, New York: W.W. Norton.

Singh, A. (1995) 'How Did East Asia Grow So Fast?: Slow Progress Towards an Analytical Consensus', UNCTAD Discussion Papers, No. 97, February.

Singh, K. (1999) *The Globalization of Finance: A Citizen's Guide*, London: Zed.

Sklair, L. (1991) *Sociology of the Global System*, New York: Harvester Wheatsheaf.

—— (1997) 'Social Movements for Global Capitalism: The Transnational Capitalist Class in Action', *Review of International Political Economy* 4, 3(Autumn): 514–538.

—— (1998) 'Social Movements and Global Capitalism', in Fredric Jameson and Masao Miyoshi (eds) *The Cultures of Globalization*, Durham, NC: Duke University Press.

Skocpol, T. (ed.) (1985) *Bringing the State Back In*, Cambridge: Cambridge University Press.

Snodgrass, D. (1980) *Inequality and Economic Development in Malaysia*, New York: Oxford University Press.

Sprague, J. (1999) 'Mind Your Language!', *Asiaweek* 30 July.

Stiglitz, J. (1989) 'Financial Markets and Development', *Oxford Review of Economic Policy* 5(4): 55–68.

—— (1999) 'More Instruments and Broader Goals: Moving Towards the Post-Washington Consensus', The Wider Annual Lecture, Helsinki.

Strange, S. (1995) 'The Defective State', *Daedalus* 124(2): 55–74.

—— (1998) *Mad Money: When Markets Outgrow Governments*, Manchester: Manchester University Press.

Sussangkarn, C., Flatters, F. and Kittiprapas, S. (1999) *Social Impacts of the Asian Economic Crisis in Thailand, Indonesia, Malaysia and the Philippines*, Bangkok: Thailand Development Research Institute.

Sutlive, Jr, Vinson H. (1992) *Tun Jugah of Sarawak: Colonialism and Iban Response*, Kuala Lumpur: Fajar Bakti.

Tabak, F. (1996) 'The World Labour Force', in Terence K. Hopkins *et al.* (eds) *The Age of Transition: Trajectory of the World System 1945–2025*, London: Zed, pp. 87–116.

Tan Chee Beng (1997) 'The Badəng', in Lok Kok Wah Francis (ed.) *Sabah and Sarawak: The Politics of Development and Federalism, Kajian Malaysia, Journal of Malaysian Studies*, Special Issue, Vol. XV, Nos 1&2.

Tanner, L. (1999) *Open Australia*, Sydney: Pluto Press.

The Sun 5 October 1998; 9 June 1999.

The Sunday Magazine 13 December 1998.

The Sunday Star 14 July 1996.

UNCTAD (1994) *World Investment Report*, Geneva: United Nations.

—— (1998) *World Investment Report*, Geneva: United Nations Conference on Trade and Development.

—— (1998) *Trade and Development Report 1998*, Geneva: United Nations.

UNDP (1994) *Human Development Report 1994*, New York: Oxford University Press.

—— (1998) *Human Development Report 1998*, New York: Oxford University Press.

—— (1999) *Human Development Report 1999*, New York: Oxford University Press.

Wade, R. (1990) *Governing the Market*, Princeton, NJ: Princeton University Press.

—— (1999) 'The Asian Crisis and the Politics of Free Capital Mobility', Paper presented at Conference on Responding to Financial Crises, Taiwan Institute of Economic Research, Taipei.

Wade, R. and Veneroso, F. (1998) 'The Asian Crisis: The High Debt Model Versus the Wall Street-Treasury-IMF Complex', *New Left Review* 228: 3–23.

Wallerstein, I. (1999) *The End of the World As We Know It: Social Science for the Twenty-First Century*, Minneapolis: University of Minnesota Press.

Waltz, K.N. (1999) 'Globalization and Governance', *Political Science and Politics* 32(4): 693–700.

Waters, M. (1995) *Globalization*, London: Routledge.

Weber, M. (1948) 'Politics as a Vocation', in H.H. Gerth and C.W. Mills (eds) *From Max Weber: Essays in Sociology*, London: Routledge & Kegan Paul, pp. 77–128.

Wee Chong Hui (1995) *Sabah and Sarawak in the Malaysia Economy*, Kuala Lumpur: S.A. Majeed.

Weiss, L. (1998) *The Myth of the Powerless State*, Ithaca, NY: Cornell University Press.

Wertheim, W.F. (1964) 'Betting on the Strong?', in *East-West Parallels: Sociological Approaches to Modern Asia*, The Hague: W. van Hoeve, pp. 259–277.

World Bank (1993) *The East Asian Miracle*, New York: Oxford University Press.

—— (1995) *World Development Report 1995: Workers in an Integrating World*, New York: Oxford University Press.

—— (1998) *World Development Report*, New York: World Bank/Oxford University Press.

—— (1999) *Knowledge for Development*, New York: Oxford University Press.

Yang, Y.H. (1994) 'The Financial System and Financial Policy in Taiwan: Lessons for Developing Countries', Occasional Paper Series No. 9410, Chung-Hua Institute for Economic Research, Taipei.

Yearley, S. (1996) *Sociology, Environmentalism, Globalization: Reinventing the Globe*, London: Sage.

You, J.I. (1995a) 'A Reflection on the Korean Miracle: Toward a New Concept of Development', *Ritsumeikan Journal of International Relations and Area Studies* 8.

—— (1995b) 'Income Distribution and Growth in East Asia', Paper presented at the UNCTAD Conference on Income Distribution and Development, Geneva, December.

Zawiah Yahya (1994) *Resisting Colonialist Discourse*, Bangi: Universiti Kebangsaan Malaysia.

Zeitlin, I.M. (1984) *Ancient Judaism: Biblical Criticism from Max Weber to the Present*, Cambridge: Polity Press.

Index